"*Frugal Families* is filled with the kinds of 'must-have' resources and accumulated wisdom every young family should keep at its fingertips."

—**Sue Gregg**
SueGreggCookbooks

"Authoritative, timely, and chock-full of bite-sized information, *Frugal Families* will help maxed-out parents stretch the family budget in ways they never thought possible."

—**Mike Yorkey**
Author, *21 Days to a Thrifty Lifestyle*

Books by Jonni McCoy

Frugal Families

Miserly Meals

Miserly Moms

Frugal Families

MAKING THE MOST OF YOUR HARD-EARNED MONEY

Jonni McCoy

BETHANYHOUSE
MINNEAPOLIS, MINNESOTA

Frugal Families (Second Edition)
Copyright © 1998, 2003
Jonni McCoy

Cover design by Andrea Boven

Published by Bethany House Publishers
A Ministry of Bethany Fellowship International
11400 Hampshire Avenue South
Bloomington, Minnesota 55438
www.bethanyhouse.com

Printed in the United States of America by
Bethany Press International, Bloomington, Minnesota 55438

Library of Congress Cataloging-in-Publication Data

McCoy, Jonni.
    Frugal families : making the most of your hard-earned money / by Jonni
McCoy. — 2nd ed.
        p.   cm.
Includes bibliographical references and index.
    ISBN 0-7642-2614-2 (pbk.)
    1. Consumer education. 2. Home economics. I. Title.
TX335 .M382   2003
640—dc21   2002152386

ACKNOWLEDGMENTS

I would like to acknowledge the valuable help given to me by my friends Kat and Craig Osten in helping me do research for this book.

DEDICATION

I dedicate this book to my precious family:

*To my husband, Beau,
for his research, valuable support,
and constant belief in me,*

*and to my children, Jeremy and Jessica,
for their patience and interest.*

JONNI McCOY holds a Bachelor of Arts degree in Speech Communication from the University of California at Santa Barbara. Prior to motherhood, she spent ten years as a senior buyer and supervisor for electronics firms such as Apple Computer and National Semiconductor. She presents seminars on living for less to women's groups and other conferences. She has been practicing her frugal ways since 1991. Jonni has appeared on several television and radio programs, including the *Gayle King Show, The 700 Club, FamilyLife Today,* and the *Dick Staub Show.* She has also been featured in magazines, including *Family Circle, Good Housekeeping,* and *Woman's Day.* Jonni and her husband, Beau, make their home in Colorado Springs, Colorado, where they homeschool their children.

CONTENTS

Frugality Run Amuck

It is a great mistake to suppose that economy consists in buying the poorest articles and in making the table unattractive.

—*Buckeye Cookery*, 1881

$ $ $

Frugality has been the greatest tool I have ever discovered. It made it possible for me to stay at home and raise my children. It taught me how to spend less on items so that I could use the extra money for more important matters. It opened my eyes to the option of quitting my job.

When I embarked on my frugal journey, I worked hardest on my daily budget needs (groceries, utilities, etc.). When I got those under control, I began to think about those occasional expenses such as vacations, cars, home appliances, etc. I needed to get a grip on how to save and shop wisely for those as well. This book was written to help your family tackle some of those expenditures.

All of my suggestions are things I have tried, and nowhere will I ask you to spend time on insignificant activities. Sadly, frugality has received a bad reputation through the years. It's understandable how people could get the wrong impression about frugality. We hear of frugal people suggesting uses for dryer lint (I think it belongs in the garbage can) or reusing plastic wrap. Some frugal folks wear stained and torn clothing in the name of frugality. Others refuse to tip waiters in the name of being frugal. These are examples of frugality run amuck: of being cheap, not frugal.

True frugality should be a means to an end. It should have something to show for itself. I don't see it as endless energy spent on minor savings. To decide if a frugal activity is worth my time, I figure out what the savings will be for my time spent on that activity. I am frugal so I can be at home with my kids. I want to spend as much time with them as possible, so my frugality must be carefully chosen.

We must choose how we fill our days. Nobody can do it all. Find the activities that save you the most money and drop the rest. Your family and friends are more important. Play with your kids. Plant a garden. Read a book.

CHAPTER ONE

Getting Home

No job can compete with the responsibility of shaping and molding a new human being.

—Dr. James Dobson

$ $ $

$\mathcal{S}$urvey statistics show that 80 percent of parents believe that one parent should be at home with the kids. Additionally, 75 percent of working women claim that they place family over work.[1] Despite this information, during the past twenty years, the number of two-income families has increased by 60 percent.[2] What makes these families live contrary to their beliefs? Misunderstandings about money: how much is needed and how to use it.

We lived with this same dichotomy for several years. As a senior buyer at Apple Computer I had a great career that I didn't want to give up. I liked the extra income, and I enjoyed the personal challenge that the job brought me. But I also felt the tug of wanting to do a better job as a mom and wife at home. Adding to my struggle were the fatigue and stress that come with trying to be good in both worlds. Finally, after three and a half years, I decided to take the plunge and quit. Since I made over 50 percent of our joint income, this was going to be tough. Living in the third most expensive area in the nation (San Francisco Bay area) didn't help things either.

We originally didn't think it could be done and planned to move into the less-expensive suburbs. But I wanted to stay where we were. We were able to keep our home and our cars while adding another child to the family.

I learned to cut back in ways I never knew one could. I cut our grocery bill in half and kept our clothing expenses down to $350 for the year. We didn't eat out or go on a vacation until we got the budget balanced. I cut every area of our budget to reach my goal of staying home. And it worked.

THE PROBLEM

Many women want to stay home, but they are afraid of what being frugal will do to them or their families. They have visions of making disgusting choices or fear severe deprivation. I feared these things too. Living frugally didn't come naturally for me. As a child I spent six years overseas with my parents, where we lived an upper-class lifestyle. We had five servants and traveled all over the world to exotic locations. Later my parents graciously paid for my four years at a university. I was accustomed to good things. But I took the plunge because of my desire to be an at-home mom. I am living proof that living frugally doesn't mean giving up your sense of class.

A national survey was conducted among several national mothers' organizations, asking for the main reasons parents wanted to be at home. Here are the top eight reasons given:

- We felt it was the best way to raise our child.
- We didn't want to miss our child's childhood.
- We wanted to raise our child with our values.
- My emotional attachment was too strong to leave my child.
- My workload was too heavy.
- My work schedule was too inflexible.
- We couldn't find adequate childcare.
- We couldn't afford adequate childcare.[3]

Some experts fear that the fatigue, stress, and alienation that come with both parents working is causing a social crisis in America. They feel that the isolation people are experiencing is causing a breakdown in communities and families. I have a friend who is a student advisor at a university. She has seen a drastic difference in the students who have enrolled during the past five years as compared to those of fifteen years ago. In her opinion, today's students are immature and lack most life skills. She credits the lack of an at-home parent as a main cause.

Many family counselors have been quoted as saying that children need more than the best that a caregiver can provide. According to Dr. Jay Belsky, a Penn State psychologist who conducted extensive research on the effects of childcare, babies who don't form an attachment with one main provider will have less self-control and will be less cooperative as they mature. Behavioral problems tend to plague these children as they get older.[4] Other researchers have found that children who grow up in daycare may do better academically, but they tend to be more hyperactive, less curious, less responsive to adults, less altruistic, and have poor relationships. And, unfortunately, most working mothers have children under the age of six. These children need their moms, especially during those early years.

Only you can decide whether or not the conclusions made by these experts are true for your family. Some parents have effectively balanced their working and at-home lives. Some may yearn for a more peaceful lifestyle and more time with their children. If the latter is your situation, there may be a way for you to come home.

COST OF WORKING

I discussed the cost of working in my book *Miserly Moms* (Bethany House, 2001) but felt it was important enough to repeat a portion of the information here. There is a huge misconception about what we actually bring home when we work and whether going to work is the best choice.

Surprisingly, many have found that having one person at home actually costs them less than having both spouses working—and can be less stressful. This may sound strange, but I found it to be true. When I chose to stay at home with my children, we assumed we would have to move to a less-expensive suburb to compensate for the 50 percent loss of income. But when I couldn't go through with the move (emotionally), we were in a pickle. Same house, same lifestyle, but half the money. Even though I wanted to be at home full time, out of desperation I looked at working part time.

It was then that I realized how much working costs.

Financial experts have calculated the cost of working at any-where from $9 to $25 per hour. I was stunned when I learned this! That meant that a job paying $10 per hour could provide only $1 for every hour worked. I read about one man who earned $28 per hour, but he only saw $2.65 per hour after his working costs. I have talked with several people who, upon calculating their cost of working, realized they were *paying* for the privilege of working!

Here are some of the expenses figured into these experts' cal-culations:

- childcare
- taxes (local, federal, state)
- commuting fees (tolls, parking, etc.)
- gasoline and mileage
- car insurance (extra car, nicer car for the job, commuter vs. leisure rating, etc.)
- clothes (new fashions, cleaners, accessories, etc.)
- gifts for co-workers
- fast-food lunches and breakfasts
- convenience foods at home
- extra eating out
- occasional housekeeping help
- hair care

Every person has a different cost of working. Some people have several children in daycare, while others have no children. Some commute many miles to work, while others ride a bike. Some can wear casual clothes to work, while others are required to dress in suits. Some are in a higher tax bracket than others. With this list, you can factor your own cost of working.

We found we could save plenty with my staying at home. Many expenses disappeared that we had not planned on. First, our taxes went down into a lower bracket without my salary. Second, our food costs went down. We ate out less (eating out typically costs six times more than making it at home) and cut our grocery bill by 60 percent with shopping and cooking changes. Third, I had time to shop for sale prices on all items from food to clothing to furniture. Fourth, we needed fewer work-related items (salon haircuts, new clothes, dry cleaning, and office gifts). And finally, we needed less "stress buster" entertainment.

$\mathcal{M}$AKING THE CHOICE

Some parents truly are unable to cut their income any further and circumstances require that both parents work. I have met many who are "stuck" there, and my heart goes out to them as they juggle their lifestyle. Many parents ache for their kids as they go off to work and rejoice when they reunite in the evening. These folks are doing what they can.

Other families have been able to follow their convictions. There are three women whose stories of personal cost are worth knowing about. These ladies made major sacrifices in order to stay at home. One is Helen Jackson, a NASA employee, who was slated to be the first black woman astronaut. She graduated from Johns Hopkins University as an astronautic electronics engineer and was in line for space travel. But she watched her kids flounder. They did poorly in school and had social problems. They needed the stability of a parent at home. Helen gave up her career to be there for them and they responded. She has never looked back in regret. The career she chose of molding those kids was more important to her.

Another woman I know wanted very much to be at home full time. She had been a working parent for four years, and she and her husband had accumulated $42,000 in debt. She took the plunge for the sake of her child and is living frugally in order to do so. The family is not incurring any further debt and is slowly paying down the existing debt. Most families would have chosen two incomes in order to pay down the debt.

Last, but not least, is a friend who has four children. Her husband works for a low wage and receives no benefits. They also pay child support for his son from a previous marriage. They live meagerly but happily. They have their stresses over finances, but they know it's better for her to be at home right now. So sacrifices are made—for now. They know it gets better with time.

Once you are willing to make some changes, the plunge doesn't seem so overwhelming. The challenge is being willing. Amazingly, 69 percent of all parents say they want a simpler life.[5]

What is keeping people at work when they want to be at home? The biggest concern is money. Many fear the loss of one job, so the other parent works, "just in case." Many can't bear the idea of being at home all day with little kids. Other reasons are more complicated. Here are samplings of the main reasons parents give for remaining at work:

Society

There is an unfortunate lack of identity for the at-home mom. Many ask her, "That's *all* you do?" Many moms struggle with the "shelving" of their education, training, or job skills. The at-home mom has no title, promotions, raises, or pats on the back. Of the moms surveyed, 28 percent said the hardest part of quitting was the loss of professional status.[6] Not surprisingly, affluent moms go back to work as often as low-income moms. It's not just for the money.

If a lack of identity is an issue, volunteer work can give that immediate sense of approval. Raising a child should be seen as a ministry, not as something that gets in the way of our careers or other interests. Even though the moms surveyed said they had a hard time with the loss of job status, 35 percent said they felt more at peace with themselves after quitting.[7]

Spousal Rejection

A spouse who is at home is often taken for granted by the working spouse. Of the spouses surveyed, most were supportive of the other spouse's decision to leave work.[8] But 24 percent said they were unhappy, concerned, or outright unsupportive.

The working spouse may be clueless as to the day-to-day stress of an at-home parent. Communicating with your spouse about the changes and new lifestyle is essential. Your identity in his mind will change. And it is essential that the at-home mom get reinforcement from other moms or outside involvements.

Loneliness

The loss of a peer group at work and the routine of being at home scares many people. Getting involved in a community college, kids' play group, club, church, or volunteer group can provide that new support group. To help you get started, you'll find a list of some support groups at the end of this chapter.

Just in Case

The fear of one spouse losing a job or the instability of one spouse's income will keep many couples both working. Some husbands, for example, have seasonal jobs, contracting jobs that come and go, or commission-based income. Some women fear that if they ever divorce or are widowed they would need to be working in order to survive. These can be real fears. Only they can decide if they should listen to the fears or step out in faith. But many have left the work force realizing that their job is to care for the children and the home.

Job Mobility

Many fear they will never be able to return to their current level in their career. Don't let fear of the future interfere with what you believe is right for today. Besides, you may change. When you return to work, you may have different interests. And the skills you acquire at home or doing volunteer work may be useful in a future career.

Cost of Living

The cost of living is about the same as it was ninety years ago[9] (factoring in adjustments for inflation). We just want more than our elders did. We want it bigger, faster, and more convenient. Perhaps this statistic helps explain a trend: the average American woman spends six hours per week shopping but only forty minutes per week playing with her kids. The kids want your time, not your money or better things.

Unstructured Days

Many fear the day-to-day drudgery of caring for kids, diapers, and toys. They see endless days that drag on and flow into one another. This could happen unless you create a structure for yourself. Get up early, exercise, read, and have a set time for certain types of activities with the kids, for outings, personal hobbies, and so forth.

TAKING THE PLUNGE

Taking the plunge into the at-home world can be scary. But, in my opinion, it is worthwhile to those who desire it. I have heard numerous success stories of people who overcame obstacles and quit their jobs. The rewards they received often exceeded their expectations. I have dedicated an entire chapter to some of these stories in *Miserly Moms* and on my Web site (*www.miserlymoms.com*).

If you are going to take the plunge into the "nonworking" world (which is a misnomer), you must do a few things first. Without these steps, you might be tempted to give up in frustration and return to work.

- Keep your goal at the forefront of your mind. Never forget why you are making these changes. You will need this reminder on those hard days.
- Live on one income before you quit. Reduce expenses as though one spouse were at home, and live like that for three to six months. Save any extra income you can. You need to know the obstacles and also save for unforeseen problems down the road.
- Learn all you can on how to trim the budget before you have to. Read and then read some more on the topic. In *Miserly Moms,* I explain how we cut our income and expenses by 50 percent. There are specific tips on every area of our household budget, including how we dramatically reduced our grocery bill. Other books on the topic are listed in the Resources at the back of this book.

SUPPORT GROUPS

- La Leche League: Nursing moms support group
  1400 N. Meacham Rd.
  Schaumburg, IL 60168-4079

(847) 519-7730
http://lalecheleague.org
- Mothers and More (formerly FEMALE): Support group for mothers who left a career
P.O. Box 31
Elmhurst, IL 60126
(630) 941-3553
www.mothersandmore.com
- Hearts at Home: A nondenominational Christ-centered professional organization for mothers at home or those who want to be
900 West College
Normal, IL 61761
(309) 888-MOMS
www.hearts-at-home.org
- International Moms' Club: Supports at-home mothers
25371 Rye Canyon Rd.
Valencia, CA 91355
www.momsclub.org
- MOPS International (Mothers of Preschoolers): Christian support group for mothers of preschoolers
P.O. Box 102200
Denver, CO 80250-2200
(800) 929-1287
www.mops.org
- Mothers at Home, Inc.: Offers a national newsletter called "Welcome Home"
9493-C Silverking Ct.
Fairfax, VA 22031
(703) 352-1072
www.familyandhome.org

RESOURCES

Burkett, Larry. *Women Leaving the Workplace: How to Make the Transition From Work to Home.* Moody Press, 1999.

Burton, Linda, Janet Dittmer, and Cheri Loveless. *What's a Smart Woman Like You Doing at Home?* Mothers at Home, 1993.

Dorn, Katie K. *From Briefcase to Diaper Bag: How I Quit My Job, Stayed*

Home With My Kids, and Lived to Tell About It. Time Books, 1995.

Field, Christine. *Coming Home to Raise Your Children: A Survival Guide for Moms.* Revell, 1995.

Fox, Isabelle. *Being There: The Benefits of a Stay-at-Home Parent.* Barron's Educational Series, 1996.

Hunter, Brenda. *Home by Choice: A Decision Every Mother Must Face.* Multnomah Books, 2000.

Lewis, Deborah S., and Charmaine C. Yoest. *Mother in the Middle: Searching for Peace in the Mommy Wars.* Zondervan, 1996.

McHugh, Jennifer, and Jeannie DeSena. *The Best of the Proverbs 31 Homemaker: Encouragement and Ideas for Wives and Mothers.* Proverbs 31 Homemaker Press, 1996.

Otto, Donna. *The Stay-at-Home Mom: For Women at Home and Those Who Want to Be.* Harvest House, 1997

Sanders, Darcie, and Martha Bullen. *Staying Home: From Full-Time Professional to Full-Time Parent.* Spencer & Waters, 2001.

Tolliver, Cindy. *At-Home Motherhood: Making It Work for You.* Resource Publication, 1994.

CHAPTER TWO

Making Money at Home

She sets about her work vigorously. . . . She sees
that her trading is profitable.

—Proverbs 31:17–18

$ $ $

$\mathscr{I}$magine you are working at home on an assignment and the children are playing quietly by themselves. You are wearing your favorite comfortable clothes and your car is still parked in your garage. You "have it all": an income, being available to your children, and your finger in the working world.

My first joy in not having to go to an office every day was the lack of need for office clothes, uncomfortable shoes, and the commute. These were a great relief to me. As temporal as those freedoms may sound, there were other, more important things I liked about working from home.

I had time to be creative with my work. I could develop plans to make things work smoother without worrying that the boss would think I was wasting time. My time was my time and I could use it as I needed. Not being "on the clock" but rather being paid by the project allowed me to use my time to the best of my abilities. This also allowed me to work more efficiently. I could get my work done in less time but still produce quality work. A supervisor who was more concerned with hours than quality didn't stifle me.

Working on projects also allowed me to focus on the type of work I loved to do. I wasn't required to do additional work that the boss needed done. This, in turn, allowed me to develop my skills and talents. That freedom allowed me to be self-sufficient in my career path. I could succeed (or fail) at a greater rate, but it would be due to my own efforts. I would not be held back by someone else's agenda for me.

Another great aspect of working from home is the flexible schedule. I could work when it was right for me. If I was feeling creative at 10:00 P.M. and not at 8:00 A.M., then I could do my work at that time. Or if the kids and I wanted to do something, I could drop the work and get back to it later. That flexibility is what attracts most people to working at home. Your time is your time: no asking permission to take a day off, no time clock for coffee breaks, no scheduling of vacations around others.

WHAT YOU GIVE UP

Remember the scenario that opened this chapter? Where you "had it all" while being at home and making money? Now add in that the children begin to fight, the baby wakes from his nap, the phone rings, and someone is at the door.

This, unfortunately, is the more realistic picture of the at-home working mom. Finding uninterrupted time to work is difficult. I know this frustration all too well. When my son was born, I wasn't ready to give up my career as a senior buyer at Apple Computer. I wanted to "have it all." While he was a baby, I was able to bring him to work for short periods. He would sleep on my lap or in his travel-size playpen while I worked. But as he grew, he became more active; bringing him to work wasn't acceptable anymore.

I worked part time in a job-share program for three years before quitting to be at home full time. Once I was at home, I still wanted to make some money, keep my finger in the professional world, and have the mental stimulation that working on a project brings. I took several free-lance assignments that allowed me to work at home. Not all were with my former employer, and not all required my past training. The assignments varied. Most of the employers were looking for someone reliable and able to follow their direction. I learned about them through word of mouth from other work-at-home moms.

At first I had a schedule for when I worked. But that didn't last long. The employer would call with last-minute questions or changes, or my son wouldn't take his nap. If my son was running around it was very hard to get much work done. I either needed to be on the phone with the client or I needed a long, uninterrupted time to think clearly. It became harder and harder to find time for either.

My choices were to stay up late to get my work done or hire a baby-sitter. Sometimes I was able to find a friend who would swap watching the kids with me. Other times I relied on a baby-sitter. And the rest of the time I worked in the evenings when my husband was available. It became a juggling act that added some stress to our lives.

Not everyone has as much difficulty as I did in juggling the work and home issues. Most of the time working at home can be a great way to make money and be more available to your children. I enjoyed the freedom of doing things that I loved, the flexibility of working for myself, and the added income. Despite the stresses, I continued to work from home. Still, before you try it, make sure you know what to expect.

Most people don't mind the trade-offs that come with working from home. They view the issues as minor inconveniences. Whether you consider them major or minor issues, be aware of them. When you work at home, here's what you might give up:

Working outside the home offers a regular paycheck that you can depend on. That in itself can be a great comfort. Having a regular income to use in budgeting can bring serenity. Employers also offer the convenience of calculating your taxes and paying them on your behalf. Having to figure your own taxes and pay quarterly estimated taxes can be a hassle. Plus, when your taxes are withheld from a paycheck, you avoid the risk of not having the taxes paid at tax time or being strapped for cash. This scenario can be life changing: no tax money means liens and foreclosures, and bankruptcies may follow.

Employment outside the home also includes paid benefits. Most employers offer some (or all) of the following: paid sick leave, paid vacation, medical insurance, dental or vision plans, and contributions to your retirement fund. This last benefit can be very valuable. If an employer is offering matching contributions to your retirement fund, the company is giving you free money. For every dollar you put aside for retirement, the employer puts in a set amount. This can add up to tens of thousands of dollars over a few years' time.

Top 10 Home Business Mistakes

1. Not doing enough research beforehand.
2. Passivity—if you are passive by nature it is best to work for someone else.
3. Poor time management.
4. Considering this to be less serious than a "traditional" job.
5. Not following the 80/20 philosophy—that 80 percent of your business comes from 20 percent of your client base. Keep those folks happy.
6. Not promoting your business frequently. Too often self-employed workers and small businesses look upon promoting themselves as an unnecessary expense rather than an essential investment.
7. Spending too freely. You may not need "high-tech," just "appropriate tech."
8. Not spending when you need to—sometimes you have to spend money to make money.
9. Not asking for help when you need it.
10. Not having a contingency plan for hard economic times. Set yourself up to go without a paycheck for at least six months while you build your business.[1]

Being employed outside the home also offers something that you can't buy: the camaraderie of other employees. Those spontaneous lunches, chats at the water cooler, and friendships that build are unique to the working environment.

Another consideration is the lack of promotion available to independent, work-at-home contractors. You will be hired for a specific purpose, and when that job is done, you may be expendable. There is little loyalty to the outside employee, and there are few opportunities for job advancement or promotions. It can also be difficult to get a raise in pay, since it's harder for you or your employer to evaluate your performance outside of the office.

*B*EFORE TAKING THE PLUNGE

If you're anything like me, the pluses outweigh the minuses, and you still want to work from home. Before you leave your job or start taking in work at home, however, consider a few things to make the journey smoother.

I mentioned the lack of uninterrupted time while I was working at home. This can be a serious predicament for the prospective working mom. We tend to think that we have a lot of time available to us, but in fact, we may not. The time we need to supervise younger children or to do household chores frequently cuts into our work time. To make an honest assessment of how much time you actually have available, conduct a time inventory. Be as detailed as you can: account for every hour. After looking over the time inventory, ask yourself where you wasted time and what could be reduced or delegated. Ask yourself if your priorities in time use are good: do you attend to the items based on importance? In order to work at home and reach your goals, your time use must reflect your priorities. You may need to say no to certain interruptions that interfere with your more important goals. You may have to ignore the phone if you know you will chat and consume your work time. You may need to give up some television viewing. You might need to schedule your errands to off-peak hours so that you can work when you need to. In order to make some of these changes, you must get the support of your family. If it affects them, they need to agree with why you are doing it.

The next thing to consider is what your real take-home pay will be. With an at-home business, you will have new financial issues. There are new taxes to pay and new deductions you can take, along with related record keeping. I will briefly cover some of these, but consider one of the books that I recommend in the resource section for more detailed information.

Your workspace at home may now be tax deductible. But if you are using the family computer, you might not be able to take the deduction. To know if you can deduct home expenses, please read the tax laws carefully (IRS publication #587, "Business Use of Your Home").

Other deductions you may be able to take are the indirect expenses in running the home. If your office qualifies as a deduction, then portions of maintaining that area may also be deductible. Expenses such as heating, a new roof, painting, and carpeting may be deductible based on the percentage of area that belongs to the workspace.

You may be able to deduct part of your auto expenses if your car is used for business. Keep a log of the mileage for each work-related trip. Those miles are deductible. Keep receipts for parking fees, toll bridges, etc., since they are fully deductible as well. Start a folder for all of the receipts for office supplies: printer paper, ink for the printer, pens, staples, postage, envelopes, telephone charges, new phone line installation fee, etc. These are deductible as office expenses if used for your work.

You will need to file estimated taxes four times per year using form 1040-ES, "Declaration of Estimated Tax." The IRS requires that you pay some portion of your taxes each quarter: January 15, April 15, June 15, and September 15. If you employ someone, you are required to obtain an employer's identification number (IRS form SS-4), pay the IRS 6.7 percent of the employee's earnings to Social Security, and perform other payroll-related services. To avoid these headaches, pay help as sub-contractors. Make sure that those people will declare their earnings to the government, since you will not. If you pay a subcontractor more than $600 per year, you need to provide that person with a form 1099.

All of these records must be kept neat and clear so that anyone could understand them. A clear record-keeping system will also make it easy to budget what you can spend. Don't make the frequent mistake that self-employed people make: spending too freely. There may not be as much money available as you think. Once you know how much your regular monthly expenses will be and what you are earning, you can see what you have available.

ASSESSING YOUR SKILLS

Now that you know how to start your business, what business will you conduct? This may already be determined. If so, have you considered how much marketing that job will require? Are you willing to do that much self-promotion? Does your job require people to visit your home? Does your neighborhood have covenants that restrict conducting a home business that has customers visiting you? Are there zoning requirements that you will need to abide by? These are just a few of the questions to ask yourself. You want to find something that you do well, that you enjoy doing, and that people will pay for.

To help direct you toward your ideal job, consider:

1. What do you like doing with your free time?
2. Do you want to sell a product or a service?
3. Do you have any hobbies that are marketable? Crafts, piano playing/teaching, etc.
4. Are you technical or imaginative? Being imaginative may eliminate detail-oriented jobs like bookkeeping, and open up jobs such as desktop publishing.

Ask friends and family what they think you would be good at. Sometimes others know us better than we know ourselves!

There are two types of work that one can do from home: selling services or selling products. Services can be anything you are good at that others will pay for. If you have training in something such as accounting, bookkeeping, or graphic arts, then sell that service. But even if you don't have training, you can still provide a service.

The first job I had right out of college was as an accounts payable clerk. I had a degree in speech communications and no experience. I hated the job and quit after eight months. Right after I quit, I started my own at-home business and called it Presentations Unlimited. I wanted a broad title that would allow me to do anything that came my way. I went back to the bank that I had worked for and asked what projects they might need help with. First, I worked in the office with some mailing campaigns. Then I was asked to help come up with ideas for training the bank tellers on what a debit card was. I had a blast thinking of silly ways to educate. This lasted for about ten months, and then I was no longer needed. I didn't have any special training or experience, but I was hired because I started talking to people, letting them know me and the things I could offer: my time, my creativity, and my flexibility. The moral of this story: A service may take no training but can provide a solution to what you see a need for.

At one time I tried selling products instead of services. Selling a product can take two paths: selling your own homemade products or selling a company's products. Whichever you do, it takes marketing skills to make this type of home business work. If you choose to sell your own products, you can find avenues locally such as craft fairs and bazaars. Or you can ask stores to carry your items on consignment (they don't buy the item from you, but take a commission from the sold items). Selling on the Internet is also possible. But self-promotion is the key element you need to make this type of home business work. You have to create a market for the item as well as sell yourself as reputable and reliable.

To reduce the amount of self-promotion needed, some people choose a product that already has a reputation. They become independent consultants selling a well-known company's products, such as Avon, Pampered Chef, Mary Kay, or Discovery Toys. The advantage is that you only have to find customers, not sell the reputation of the company. The downside is that you are limited to a certain percentage of profit and cannot promote the business in ways that you might if you were promoting your own product.

I tried selling Discovery Toys. I did very well and made it to the manager level. I quit right after that. My success was limited if it was measured by my personal efforts—I could never earn more than a flat percentage of my sales. To make more I had to become a manager. But then my earnings were not based on my performance but were measured by how well my underlings performed. I saw no more income for my efforts even though the managers above me, and the company, would. I wanted to be rewarded for my work.

Not every company has this incentive problem. Some are excellent to be associated with. And perhaps for some people this isn't an issue. Research is the key to making a good choice.

Whatever type of business you choose, there will be pros and cons. Talk to people who have tried various jobs. Visit craft fairs and talk to those who are selling their own wares. Most people love to discuss their business. Then talk to those who sell someone else's products. Educating yourself on the business will make your choice a happier one with fewer unpleasant surprises.

*J*OB POSSIBILITIES

accountant	cleaning	florist	party planner
aerobics	clipping	furniture	personal chef
instructor	newspapers	restoration	pet grooming
animal boarding	computer	gift baskets	pet sitter
answering service	programmer	hairstylist	photo restoration
antique repair	credit counselor	income tax	picture framing
antique sales	curtain making	preparation	proofreader
artist	data processing	investment	resell used goods
auto repair	daycare	counselor	resumé service
balloon delivery	desktop publishing	jewelry repair	shopping service
bookkeeping	disc jockey for	landscaping	speech therapy
bridal consultant	parties	lawn care	technical writer
cake decorator	dog training	manicurist	transcriber
calligraphy	dog walking	medical claims	travel agent
carpet cleaning	doll making	assistant	tutor
catering	dressmaking/	mobile car wash	writer
ceramics	alterations	organizer	

*M*YSTERY SHOPPING

Mystery shopping has become a popular activity for many at-home moms. In many cases it provides little or no income but provides free dining out, activities, or product. Because of its recent popularity, let's look at ways to do it successfully.

Companies will pay for information about their store's service. That's why they hire mystery-shopping companies to find people like you and me. And they pay us to shop! What could be cooler? Even though it is great to be paid to shop, mystery shopping can leave you overworked and underpaid if you aren't careful about your time and the assignments.

Different types of mystery-shopping companies exist. Some are for restaurants and some are for retail stores. Some pay flat fees for the job while a few pay by the hour. Some are independent companies that the retailer hires, and some pay the shoppers directly from corporate headquarters.

I have been a mystery shopper for several types of companies and experienced the upside and downside of this profession, learning what types of jobs to take and which companies to avoid. I hope you benefit from my experiences.

My first job was with Domino's Pizza. Assigned to a specific store, I was required to buy a medium or large pizza from it once per month. I was reimbursed a flat fee of $8 for the pizza, which usually amounted to 90 percent of the actual cost. I filled out a one-page form each time and rated the delivery time, the delivery person's manner and dress, and the pizza's quality and appearance. After almost a year, I became tired of pizza from just one company. The benefit was that I got nearly free food for my work.

Subsequent restaurant chain assignments included an Italian restaurant, Ruby Tuesday, and Texas Roadhouse. These had similar payment policies. On average, the amount of the fee fed two to three people from their menu.

Whom to Call If You've Been Scammed
Federal Trade Commission
(877) 382-4357 or *www.ftc.gov*
National Fraud Information Center
(800) 876-7060 or *www.fraud.org*
The FBI has a clearinghouse for online frauds
www.ifccfbi.gov
Your local Better Business Bureau
www.bbb.org
Your state attorney general

I then wanted to generate income for my time instead of almost-free food. So I signed with a company called Courtesy Counts, which was hired by several retailers to evaluate their stores and employees. I was assigned to shop at Gart Sports. Each shop took about two hours to complete, including the time it took to fill out the eight-page form. I was asked to go to a specific department of a specific store and have an employee explain the different brands and types of a specific item. Next, I was to buy a specific item from a different department. Then (this was the part I hated) I had to come back to the store in twenty minutes and return that same item. Each of these interactions had to be written about in great detail. For this I was paid $16. The company was difficult to work for. If the form wasn't filled out to their expectations, they wouldn't pay—anything.

As you can see, most of the jobs for restaurants pay for part of the food. So if you enjoy eating out, the work is worth the fee. If you prefer to be paid cash for your time, plenty of those jobs are out there too. But keep in mind that the assignments are sporadic;

you shouldn't rely on this type of work for regular income.

How do you find these jobs? First, be careful of the scams! Many companies ask for upfront money to simply apply with their shopping organization. Avoid these. There are plenty of reputable ones that ask for no money. When you apply, you will fill out an application. They will contact you when there is an assignment in your area. There is no limit as to the number of organizations you can sign up with.

To find some mystery-shopping companies, search the Internet using the key words *mystery shopping, secret shopper,* or *mystery shopper.* Below are a few companies that I have heard good things about, but by no means are these the only ones! For a thorough list of mystery-shopping companies and what type of companies they service, visit *www.volition.com.*

- Shop'n Chek, Inc.
  www.shopnchek.com
  (800) 669-6526
- Reality Check
  www.rcmysteryshopper.com
  (800) 550-4469
- Secret Shoppe
  www.mysteryshop.com
  (800) 781-7467

$\mathcal{A}$VOIDING SCAMS

It's never as easy as the ads sound. Few of us can make $1,000 in our spare time. If it were that easy, we'd all be doing it. The scams prey on those yearning to be at home and make money at the same time.

Some of these companies offer you a list of other companies that might consider hiring an outside employee. The fee (usually about $50) may provide a list that is helpful. But I have found that most employers are looking for highly skilled consultants, or they prefer to hire consultants that they know are reliable—probably ex-employees wanting to work at home. Other jobs offered to the stay-at-home person are menial labor: envelope stuffing/folding, making hundreds of the same craft item, sewing hundreds of doll outfits, reading e-mails, or doing surveys or medical billing. Some are actually illegal pyramid schemes. Many require expensive equipment to be purchased upfront. Most of these offers are too good to be true, and the companies offering them are the only ones making money.

What to Watch For

Unbelievable promises
Unwilling to offer references that you can contact
No refund policy
Claim that it is "perfectly legal"
No regular salary
Requires upfront money
Requires no experience

Finally, before starting your endeavor, try your hand at your new career on the side before quitting your current job altogether. Let it be a supplement to your income before you rely on it 100 percent.

RESOURCES

Arden, Lynie. *The Work-at-Home Source Book.* Live Oak Publishing, 1996.

Brabec, Barbara. *Homemade Money: How to Select, Start, Manage, Market, and Multiply the Profits of a Business at Home.* Better Way Books, 1997.

Edwards, Paul, and Sarah Edwards. *The Best Home Businesses for the 21st Century.* Jeremy P. Tarcher, 1999.

———. *Working From Home.* Jeremy P. Tarcher, 1999.

Elyer, David R. *The Home Business Bible.* John Wiley & Sons, 1994.

Hanania, David. *Home Business Made Easy.* PSI-Research/Oasis Press, 1998.

Hicks, Tyler G. *199 Great Home Businesses You Can Start and Succeed in for Under $1,000.* Prima Publishing, 1999.

Huff, Priscilla Y. *101 Best Home-Based Businesses for Women.* Prima Publishing, 1998.

Levinson, Jay. *555 Ways to Earn Extra Money.* Henry Holt, 1991.

Partow, Donna. *Homemade Business: A Woman's Step-by-Step Guide to Earning Money at Home.* Focus on the Family, 1999.

CHAPTER THREE

Inexpensive Family Time

*A home is a kingdom of its own in the midst of
the world, a stronghold amid life's storms and
stresses, a refuge, even a sanctuary.*

—Dietrich Bonhoeffer

$ $ $

*H*ey, Mom! I'm bored! What's there to do?" is a common cry
in many homes. It can send shivers up your spine. But keeping
kids busy doesn't have to cost a great deal. With a little creativity,
most kids can be kept active for very little cost. And they love the
time you will spend with them.

Before the invention of the Jet Ski and amusement parks,
there were fun-filled days that families spent together. Social inter-
action was actually taught by parents to their children so they
could know the skill of entertaining others. There used to be
books of parlor games and other distractions. Those books are still
available if you want to pursue that type of fun. New (and used)
books on the subject can be found in most bookstores or in online
bookstores. I did a search for "parlor games" on Amazon.com
and several books appeared. Web sites are also available with
detailed descriptions of many parlor games. One site that offers
many descriptions is *www.thevictorianemporium.net/games.html.* And
you'll find more recent books with activities, crafts, and other
inexpensive family pastimes at your local library.

More importantly, spending time with our family members can
provide something far more valuable than merely a way to keep

them busy. Raising a family is more than clothes, food, and education. Parents are mentors, advisors, mediators, counselors, and above all, friends. It is on this friendship that the other foundations are built. We must first become friends before our children will come to us for advice. But that friendship cannot happen unless there is time spent together outside of the daily responsibilities of life. Sometimes that means planning for those times to happen so that they don't get forgotten in the rush of daily life.

Some families plan one special night per week for the family to do something together. Planning may be the only way to make it happen. What you do as a family should be determined by what your family's interests are. Some families play games, while others may discuss history or politics. Some share a common interest in a craft or hobby and work on that together. Others like sports and may attend a sporting event, watch one on television, or organize a family game in the yard or park. Others like outings and therefore visit museums, zoos, or historical sites. And some prefer to do a service project together such as taking food to a shelter or visiting a homebound neighbor or nursing home resident.

I have chosen a few of our family's favorite pastimes to share with your family. We hope they offer some suggestions on how to stay close to one another and have fun at the same time. They are simple and fun to do. Try out some of these ideas with your family:

- Make face paint together and take turns drawing on one another's faces. (Face paint base: 1 teaspoon cornstarch, ½ teaspoon facial cold cream or vegetable shortening, ½ teaspoon water mixed together. For different colors, divide the base and add food coloring. Use a cotton swab to apply the face paint.)
- Have a paper-airplane-making contest. Get some books from the library on different styles.
- Have a game night. Make some popcorn and enjoy some of the old classic board games.
- Take a picnic to the park. In the winter, have an indoor picnic with a tablecloth on the floor.
- Find a classic movie at the library and watch it together.
- Have an old-fashioned taffy pull. Pull it together and see how far you can stretch it.

- Make a gingerbread house together. Let everyone pick his or her own decorating medium for the house (jelly beans, wafers, etc). Or let each person take a section of the house and do it his or her way.
- Have the kids put on a magic show for the family.
- Visit some local attractions, such as factory tours, concerts, or museums. Many have a free day.
- Ride the public transit around town.
- Go miniature golfing.
- Do a jigsaw puzzle together.
- Have a water balloon fight.
- Make sidewalk chalk (plaster of paris mixed with food coloring, poured into small paper cups) and create a work of art.
- Have a treasure hunt or scavenger hunt.
- Make beanbags from scraps of fabric and dried beans or rice.
- Make a craft together and take it to a convalescent center.
- Read aloud to one another.
- Start a secret pal program at home. Draw names and get busy: write letters, give gifts, do your pal's chores, etc.
- Make sand art together. Use empty baby food jars and colored salt ("grate" colored chalk onto sandpaper and mix the dust with salt).
- Make and fly kites.
- Go roller-skating or ice-skating. Most rinks have a weekly family night that costs less.
- Make card houses and see whose will stay up the longest.
- Create a progressive story together.
- Learn to juggle together.
- Make your own trivia cards for Trivial Pursuit. Use questions that only the family would know the answer to.
- Play kick the can.
- Have a car-making contest with Legos.
- Volunteer as a family in a soup kitchen, rescue mission, or other local ministry.
- Learn origami (Japanese paper folding) together.
- Take a virtual tour of world-famous museums:
  British Museum (London, England): *www.thebritishmuseum.ac.uk/world/world.html*
  Louvre (Paris, France): *www.louvre.fr/louvrea.htm*

Cave of Chauvet-Pont-D'Arc (cave paintings in France): *www.culture.gouv.fr/culture/arcnat/chauvet/en/*

Smithsonian Institution: *www.si.edu,* then *activity/planvis/museums/i-sib.htm*

National Air and Space Museum: *www.nasm.si.edu/*

National Museum of African Art: *www.nmafa.si.edu/*

National Museum of American History: *www.americanhistory.si.edu/ve/index.htm*

National Museum of Natural History: *www.mnh.si.edu/*

National Museum of the American Indian: *www.si.edu/nmai/*

National Postal Museum: *www.si.edu/postal/*

National Zoological Park: *www.natzoo.si.edu/*

DATING YOUR SPOUSE

In addition to family time, married couples need dates and spur-of-the-moment getaways as part of their life together. These minivacations can be a source of real enjoyment and a needed break from busy routines at home and at work.

It's not necessary to spend a lot of money on these dates— many can be done for free. Before movie theaters, snowmobiles, ski lifts, or even cars, people *were* able to have fun.

My husband and I like to go on dates but usually can't afford the combined cost of a sitter, dinner at a restaurant, and movie theater tickets. So we've come up with some cheaper alternatives that are as much fun. If these don't sound as exciting as a dinner out or a movie, remember why you're going out in the first place: to be together. Following are some ideas that we have tried. To find your own, think like a tourist: read the Sunday newspaper's travel or entertainment section or read the visitor's guide put out by your city.

Inexpen$ive Date Ideas

- Go on a walk at sunset. It's beautiful and relaxing.
- Find your area's historical landmarks.
- Pick a handful of wildflowers for your partner.
- Go hiking at night under a full moon.
- Go for a bike ride.

- Visit your local zoo; take a picnic with you.
- Visit a factory that offers free tours.
- Visit crafters in their studios (pottery, glass blowers, etc.).
- Visit a nearby town that you've never explored.
- Ride the public transit of your city and see the town.
- Visit a nearby state park.
- Read a play out loud to each other.
- Attend a theater performance put on by your local college or community group.
- Rummage through a flea market.
- Attend a lecture (see local newspaper for listings).
- Visit a local art gallery.
- Do a puzzle together.
- Go to a local bookstore's readings of poetry—or just browse.
- Go stargazing. Many community colleges have free observatory nights.
- Go roller-skating or ice-skating.
- Go out for coffee and dessert instead of dinner.
- Go to matinees versus evening shows—sometimes they are half price.
- Make chocolate fondue.
- Go miniature golfing.
- Play a board game.
- Go square dancing.
- Have a taffy pull.
- Visit museums; take advantage of any free days they may offer.
- Look into free concerts in your city or town.
- Send the kids to someone's house for the night.
- Enjoy the silence.

RESOURCES

Cook, Deanna. *Family Fun Crafts: 500 Creative Activities for You and Your Kids.* Hyperion, 1997.

———. *Family Fun Parties: 100 Party Plans for Birthdays, Holidays, and Every Day (Family Fun Series, No.3).* Hyperion, 1999.

Jones, Alanna. *Team-Building Activities for Every Group.* Rec Room Pub, 1999.

Kneeland Pickett, Beth. *50 Nifty Things to Do After School.* RGC Publishing, 1995.

Kuffner, Trish. *The Toddler's Busy Book.* Meadowbrook Press, 2000.

Weisner, Canadace. *Let's Get Going: The Step-by-Step Guide to Successful Outings With Children.* General Distribution Services, 2001.

CHAPTER FOUR

Holidays With a Frugal Flare

*Tradition is not just what we receive, it is what
we create with our own hands and then hand
over, the ties we make with past and future.*

—Marcia Falk, *Heartstrings of Laughter and Love*

$ $ $

*I*f there's one theme I hope I've gotten across in my books,
it's that being frugal does not mean we have to do without or look
cheap. This is true in every area of our home—holidays included!
We can have a beautiful home that fills our guests with warmth
during the holidays. Here are some ideas we have used in our
home to enjoy the holidays in their grandeur and stay within our
budget.

CHRISTMAS

This is my favorite time of year. We celebrate this holiday for a
month in our home. I love the look, smells, and sounds of Christmas. The reason for the season—Jesus' birth—makes this a mean-
ingful time of year. You can tell how much I love this holiday by
how much more space I dedicate to it as compared to the other
holidays.

Decorating

To give your home a festive feel, try adding something natural
from the season. I fill a basket with pinecones and string some

simple white tree lights around and through the basket. Sometimes I spray-paint the cones gold or silver. This basket can be large and set by the front door or fireplace, or it can be small and placed in the center of a table.

Bring evergreen boughs into the house. If you don't have any evergreens in your yard, cut a lower limb off your Christmas tree and trim it so that it can be laid on the mantel, around staircase banisters, around a lamppost, or over a large framed picture. You can also purchase plastic boughs that are inexpensive and easy to use. Decorate them with small white tree lights or ribbons.

We also string tiny white lights around houseplants or window frames. And don't forget the wreaths! Make them with boughs, or wire together any type of branch (artificial or real) in a circular shape. Hang them inside or outside. The more the merrier!

What to do with all those cards that come in the mail? We turn them into part of the Christmas decorations. Sometimes we put them in a lovely basket (spray-paint an old one with gold or silver paint) with a ribbon tied to the handle. Other times we have strung a ribbon along the hallway or above the fireplace and hung the cards over the ribbon. Some people hang corkboard over a doorway and tack the cards to it. We try to reuse the cards as gift tags the next year: cut the picture on the card with pinking shears and punch a hole in one corner for the ribbon.

For the table, have the children help make items to arrange. They can wrap tiny boxes to place around an evergreen bough. Wrap a cardboard tube from a toilet paper roll with foil or white paper to make a paper angel. Cut some wings from paper and glue them to the back. Have the children draw on faces.

I put scented candles in the guest bathroom, kitchen, on the dining table, and wherever else they look inviting (if there are small children or perfume-allergic people in your home, you may want to avoid this tip).

Creating Memories

The best part about Christmas for me is the memories that we make together. There are so many things we can do to make this time of year special. I have pages and pages of ideas and have selected a few of our favorites for your family to try.

The music of this season is so special. I fill the house with Christmas songs all day (if the family will let me!). I go to the library every year and select several CDs (go early; they go fast!). My favorite is Handel's *Messiah*. I love to hear it, but most of all I love why it was written. Did you know that this oratorio is about the prophecies that led up to the Messiah's (Jesus') birth? And that the famous Hallelujah chorus celebrates the fulfilled prophecies? Research the Bible verses the songs are based on. I found a copy of a program for a performance that gave the Bible verse for which each chorus was written. It is great to read those verses as a family before listening to each song and understand what they are singing about.

Another song to research the meaning of is "The Twelve Days of Christmas." Discuss the meaning of each gift. While you are at the library researching these songs, read about Christmas traditions in other countries. It's fascinating! Also find a book on the story of the candy cane and its inventor.

Crafts are such an important part of Christmas for my daughter and me. We make ornaments, gingerbread houses, centerpieces, wreaths, and anything else we can think of. Some of our favorites are listed:

- Buy terra-cotta clay and roll it ½-inch thick and cut ornaments out with cookie cutters. Air-dry overnight. Draw faces and write names of friends with puff paint and give as gifts.
- Make cinnamon dough (1½ cups cinnamon, 1 cup applesauce, ⅓ cup white school glue) and form into ornaments or snowmen for table decorations. Let air-dry two to three days.
- Create a photo ornament of each child every year. Make the frame from funny foam, Popsicle sticks, a decorated lid from frozen juice concentrate, or even construction paper.
- Make your own Christmas cards for special people or the elderly, who will appreciate your personal touch.
- Make a snow globe. We have done it two ways: one with water and one without. With water requires a baby food jar, glitter, and a small toy for the center. Fill the jar with water and some glitter, and glue the toy to the inside of the lid (the lid will become the bottom of the globe). Once the jar is closed, hot-glue around the edges so nothing can be opened or leak. For

the waterless type, take a plastic bubble container that comes in gumball or vending machines. Find a tiny toy that fits inside the bubble. Glue the toy to the lid of the bubble. With a toothpick, dot white paint on the inside of the bubble to represent snow.

- Make your own Advent calendar: Draw twenty-five tiny (one-inch) pictures on a large piece of construction paper (or glue on pictures from old Christmas cards). Take another piece of paper the same size and cut windows where the pictures will be. Glue the corners of the paper together and let the kids open one frame per day.

Crafts aren't the only way to build memories. You could start a family journal that is written in only at Christmastime (keep it in with the decorations and bring it out each year). Write what each person wants for Christmas, how tall the children are, what their interests are that year, what they want to be when they grow up, etc.

Start a keepsake box for each child. Every year add an ornament for each of the children. The boxes can be given to them when they have their own tree.

To help the family understand and celebrate the reason for Christmas, celebrate it in a special way. Have an Advent wreath with candles to celebrate the month leading up to Christmas. Make a birthday cake for Jesus using colors and shapes to signify the uniqueness of his birthday: make a star-shaped cake; the icing can be white for purity or gold for royalty; layers of the cake can be different colors for different symbols.

Watch some classic Christmas movies together. Get some from the library (they're free or inexpensive!). Some of our favorites are *Miracle on 34th Street, A Christmas Carol,* and *Veggie Tales: The Toy That Saved Christmas.*

If getting outside is the best way for your family to bond, try a few of these Christmas activities:

- Have a Christmas caroling party. Invite the neighbors and visit your neighborhood or a nursing home. Offer warm drinks and cookies afterward.
- Visit a living nativity scene in your town.
- Adopt a family that is having a hard time financially. Deliver

food, gifts, or decorations to them. To find a family that wants this help, contact your church, Chamber of Commerce, or local charities.

- Practice Boxing Day. This holiday began in early England, according to some historians. On the day after Christmas, the churches would open their poor boxes and share the money with the poor. Later, in the Middle Ages, the gentry would wrap gifts that they didn't want and give them to their servants. This day became known as St. Stephen's Day, honoring the memory of this saint who was martyred. Use this day to give gifts to those who may not have much. Fill a box with things you aren't using and donate them to a local charity.
- Have a talent show for the family or invite the neighbors. Videotape it and show it every year.

Gifts

Gift giving shouldn't be something we dread or do with obligation. It should flow from our love for others. But sometimes our wallet stops us from showing those feelings as freely as we'd like. That doesn't mean we can't give gifts. Our family has tackled this issue a number of ways. We budget how much we want to spend on Christmas gifts and then put some of that money aside every month throughout the year so we don't get hit all at once. We have tried to encourage family members to draw names for gift giving so that the gift can be a little nicer and no guilt is felt if there isn't a gift from us to everyone. Other ideas have been to require that the gift be made by the giver and not purchased. That could include a craft, a poem, a letter of appreciation, etc. One year I made scrapbooks for each family member of major events in their life. (Use a three-ring binder, acid-free plastic sleeves, acid-free glue, and stickers on acid-free paper.) And there have been lean years when we have had to limit the amount that was spent on one another.

Making your gifts instead of buying them is a great way to save money. I make gifts throughout the year and keep them on hand. That way I am less busy during the holidays, I am less tempted to buy a last-minute item for someone, and I have gifts on hand for birthdays and other events throughout the year.

Some gift ideas require making the item at the time they are needed, such as baked fruit breads. You can bake these as regular-sized loaves or use mini baking tins and give a variety of breads. Wrap them in colored plastic wrap and tie each with a bow for added appeal.

One make-ahead idea is to make sachets from a small piece of fabric (four inches by four inches) wrapped around dried flowers or tied around a few cotton balls with a few drops of essential oil or vanilla dropped on them. Gather the four corners of the cloth and tie it closed with a ribbon.

One of my favorite gifts to make is a teacup candle. I look through thrift stores and garage sales for a decorative teacup and saucer set and find two votive candles of a complementary color to the pattern on the cup. I hot-glue the cup to the saucer, then melt the candles (in something I can throw away when done) in a double boiler over the stove (be careful not to spill wax on the stove). When the candles are melted, I remove the wick and hang it in the center of the cup from a pencil that is resting across the edges of the cup. Then pour the melted wax into the teacup and let it harden. This makes a lovely gift and can be accompanied by a bookmark or bookstore gift certificate.

Other make-ahead ideas include:

- Save seeds from your garden, fold paper into a seed packet, and give with a garden tool attached.
- Make some solid perfumes in pillboxes: melt two parts Vaseline with one part paraffin, and add a few drops of essential oil.
- Make stepping-stones from plaster of paris with handprints or shells or jewels.
- Make a pincushion jar filled with buttons, and top with a cotton-filled fabric cover on the lid.
- Make herbed vinegar by filling tall attractive jars with distilled vinegar and adding herbs from your garden. Seal the lid with hot wax.

Another idea is to present mixes, such as a soup mix, layered cookie mix in a jar, or cappuccino mix that can be made ahead and stored. I have included several mix recipes in my book *Miserly Meals* that can be presented as gift items.

Whatever gift you choose to make can be presented in a decorative fashion and given alone or combined with other gifts in a basket. Fill the gift basket with several different items that share a theme! To help you create a unique, beautiful basket I have listed a few themes below.

Finding the baskets isn't that hard: I buy them at thrift shops and garage sales. Sometimes I spray paint them gold or silver to spruce them up a bit. Then fill the bottom with straw, shredded leftover wrapping paper, confetti paper found at party stores, or a piece of cloth with the edges cut with pinking shears. Place several mixes and other theme items in the basket.

When giving mixes, I want the container to be attractive. For this purpose, I gather jars from various sources. For the smaller mixes such as spice mixes or salad dressings, I use baby food jars. I ask friends and neighbors to save them for me. For the larger jars, I look for one-quart canning jars at garage sales and thrift stores. The sealing portion of the lid needs to be new, so I purchase them separately. For a fancier jar, visit craft stores and hobby shops.

To make the jar attractive, cut a nine-inch circle of fabric, using pinking shears to finish the edges. Attach the fabric to the lid by hot-gluing it around the edge of the lid (use a glue gun). Then tie some raffia or ribbon around the lid. This way the lid can be removed and reattached without losing the decoration.

Another idea is to use small plastic bags to hold the mixes and surround them with a square piece of attractive fabric. A large bag of mix (two to three cups) would need an eleven-inch square of fabric to cover it. I use pinking shears on the edges so that hemming is not required. Wrap the bag of mix with the cloth, gather the edges together above the mix, and tie it with a ribbon.

For the mix instructions card, buy business cards made for desktop printers and print the instructions on them. Punch a hole in the corner of the card and tie it on the jar with the raffia or ribbon. For a more elegant look, use a gift card and write the instructions with a calligraphy pen.

Themed Gift Baskets

- *Italian Gift Basket*
  Spiral pasta

Pasta spoon
Spaghetti Sauce*
Italian Seasoning Mix*
Garlic bulbs
Fresh tomatoes
Cheese grater
Recipe card for a pasta dish
Colander could be the basket

- *Latte Lover's Basket*
Coffee mug
Suisse Mocha, Café Bavarian Mint, or Cappuccino Mix*
Chocolate-dipped spoon
Biscotti*
Powdered Flavored Creamer*

- *Movie Lover's Basket*
2 microwave popcorn bags
Chocolate bar
Sodas
Movie theater pass or movie rental certificate
Popcorn bowl for the basket

- *Bread Lover's Basket*
Loaf of Herb-and-Cheese Bread*
Bread mixes ready for bread machine
Wooden mixing spoon
Cutting board

- *S'mores Lover's Basket*
Graham crackers
Marshmallows
Chocolate bars
A skewer or nice twigs for roasting marshmallows
A scarf for those cold nights

- *Bath Lover's Basket*
Scented bath salts
Sea sponge
Scented candle

- *Pet Lover's Basket*
Homemade dog treats
Dog toy
Dog brush

- *College Student's Basket*
  Various snack foods
  Hot Cocoa, Suisse Mocha, Café Bavarian Mint or Cappuccino
    Mix*
  Layered Cookie Mix*
  Powdered Flavored Creamer*
  Chicken-Flavored Rice Mix*
  Prepaid phone card
  Gift certificate to gas stations
- *Car Lover's Basket*
  Red shop towels
  Goop hand cleaner
  Car-washing soap
  Sponges
  Window-washing solution
  The basket could be a bucket
- *Child's Busy Basket*
  Homemade play dough†
  Homemade Gak†
  Cookie cutters
  Sidewalk chalk†
  Bubbles†
  Crayons
  Silly Putty†
  Sand bucket as basket
- *Child's Dress-Up Box*
  Look at thrift stores for:
  Hats
  Uniforms
  Fancy dresses
  Costumes
  Costume jewelry
  Handbags
  Plastic swords
- *Teenage Girl's Basket*
  Nail polish
  Lip gloss
  Bubble bath

Scented bath salts
Key chains
- *Hunter/Camper's Basket*
  Granola
  Biscuit Mix*
  Soup Mix*
  Flavored Coffee Mix*
  Chicken-Flavored Rice Mix*
  Mug or bowl
- *Spice Basket*
  Mexican Seasoning Mix, Spaghetti Sauce Mix, or
      Italian Seasoning Mix*
  Chicken-Flavored Rice Mix*
  Wooden spoon
  The basket could be a mixing bowl
- *Get-Well Basket*
  Jar of Homemade Chicken Noodle Soup*
  Chicken-Flavored Rice Mix*
  Soup bowl
  Good book
  Vitamin C
  Kleenex tissue
  Baking Mix*

Wrapping Paper

I try to stock up at the after-Christmas sales on paper. These are usually 50–75 percent off. I also look for alternative types of paper to use. If you live near a paper factory or stationery manufacturer, they sometimes have ends of large rolls of paper to give away. Wallpaper stores have sheets of samples that make elegant-looking paper. We have made our own paper by buying white butcher paper and stamping, drawing, and hand printing on it. My grandmother used the Sunday comics and raffia—this has a country feel. She also used large pieces of fabric, trimmed the edges with pinking shears, and tied them with ribbon around gifts.

---

*These mixes can be found in *Miserly Meals*.
†These recipes can be found in *Miserly Moms*.

THANKSGIVING

Decorating

This time of year it is easy to incorporate the colors and fruits of nature in our decorating. Indian corn, colored leaves, straw, etc., can all be used to make a home more festive. I change the theme of my front door wreath by sticking branches with colored fall leaves in it.

The first area that I focus on is my table centerpiece. This can be an arrangement of Indian corn, leaves, miniature squash, and candles. Or you can be more elaborate and make some crafts to complete the arrangement. Make candle holders from apples (must be made very close to dinnertime). Make placemats from different colored leaves, stamping, and magazine cutouts laminated to construction paper. Make miniature scarecrows from baby or doll clothes: fill them with straw and have them sit on miniature pumpkins.

Have the children make name cards for each guest, complete with hand-drawn decorations. Make a list of the guests' names for them to work from. Then have them make napkin rings from toilet paper tubes: decorate them with paint, foil, stickers, etc.

Making Memories

As with Christmas, celebrating the holiday should be intertwined with understanding the reason for the day. Reading stories of the day's history not only brings us together but also helps us appreciate it more. Read about a day in the life of a Pilgrim or study the different types of Native American lifestyles from the northeast as compared to the Native Americans who live in your region. Use the public library for books on the holiday. Some of my favorites are listed in the resource section at the end of this chapter.

Create a Thanksgiving tablecloth that you can use each year. Start with a light-colored cloth (can be muslin) and cut and hem it to fit your table. Each year have guests write on the cloth with colored fabric pens. They can simply sign their name or write a brief "thank-you" note. I found my grandmother's tablecloth with this theme, and it is so special to see the names of past family members.

There are many more things we can do on Thanksgiving to learn what the Pilgrims did. Here are some of my favorites:

- Place five candy corns on each person's plate before they sit down. Explain that the kernels represent what each Pilgrim's meal ration might have been during that first winter.
- Have a paper turkey cut from construction paper on the wall. Have each family member write what he or she is thankful for on a feather (made from paper) and attach it to the turkey.
- Make cornhusk dolls.
- Make quills from feathers. Make ink from boiled walnut shells.
- Make butter together: put heavy whipping cream in a jar with one marble; seal and take turns shaking until the whey separates from the butter. Then use it at dinner.
- Have the children write a story from a Pilgrim's perspective.
- Listen to a radio drama of the story of Squanto (Focus on the Family has a great one).
- Make an acrostic poem from the word *Pilgrim* or *turkey* (or any other Thanksgiving word).
- Start a journal for Thanksgiving that will be added to each year. Have each person write what he or she is thankful for.
- Have the younger children create a book of what Thanksgiving means to them: cut out magazine pictures and glue to construction paper; tie the pages together with yarn.
- Have the older children write a pretend newspaper from the first Thanksgiving era complete with stories and "interviews."

Games are a fun way to spend this day, especially if the games are old-fashioned ones.

- Try a popcorn relay race using one large popcorn bowl and smaller bowls to carry the popcorn to the other end (tie small disposable plastic bowls to players' feet with a rubber band threaded through a hole in the bottom of the bowl). See which team has the most popcorn in its last bowl after two minutes!
- Make hoops with wire or pipe cleaners and use small sticks by which the hoop must be passed from person to person.

- Play the "hot/cold" game with a hidden picture of a turkey, but instead of saying "warmer" or "colder" gobble loudly or softly.
- Twenty questions is a great game to play: pick a topic related to Thanksgiving.
- And never underestimate the fun of a coloring contest. Use preprinted sheets to color or have children draw pictures freehand. The Internet is a great place to find coloring sheets if you prefer them preprinted. Two Web sites that offer several pictures are *www.kidsdomain.com/holiday/thanks/color.html* and *www.coloring.ws/thanksgiving.html.* Do an Internet search using keywords like "Thanksgiving coloring pages."

*E*ASTER

Easter is a time of celebration at our house. This is the day our Savior made our salvation possible by rising from the dead and leaving the tomb. Therefore, how we celebrate the day reflects that theme. But we incorporate traditional activities as well, like an egg hunt and spring crafts. Whatever you do to make this day special, our ideas should add something to your day.

Making Memories

There is so much we can learn and do to make the Easter season memorable. In addition to Easter, it is the celebration of spring, the time of Passover, and the end of Lent. We study Passover and the meaning of Lent throughout the Easter week and even go back forty days to the beginning of Lent. Look for books at your church or public library (I have recommended my favorites at the end of this chapter). Some of the themes that we cover include:

- What the Passover rituals are and how they foretell of Jesus
- What Palm Sunday is and how people celebrate it
- What Good Friday is and why it is called "good"
- What Lent is, why it is observed, and why the first day of Lent is called Ash Wednesday
- What the day before Lent is called and why it is celebrated (Fat Tuesday or, in French, *Mardi Gras*)

We make crafts that tell some of these stories. One of my favorites is an edible and fun activity that tells of the empty tomb. Take some biscuit dough that is cut into rounds and ready to bake. Place a marshmallow between two biscuit rounds and pinch the edges of the dough around the marshmallow so it is sealed inside the dough. Bake the biscuits according to the directions. When they are done and you open them, the marshmallow is gone; there is a hollow space inside, but the biscuit remained sealed!

Another craft that kids enjoy is making salt dough (there is an easy recipe for it in *Miserly Moms*). Let the kids make a tomb or complete garden surrounding the tomb. Let them put sticks in it for trees, toy soldiers, a door on the tomb (a rock or graham cracker will work), or anything else their imagination desires. We do this inside an empty shoebox.

My daughter's favorite activity for this time of year starts twelve days before Easter with our homemade version of Resurrection Eggs. Resurrection Eggs are a dozen plastic eggs housed in an egg carton, each filled with something to tell a part of the Easter story. In each egg we place something to remind us of the story along with a small piece of paper with a verse from the Bible that tells about that event. Once the eggs are completed, they can be stored for use each year or modified as you desire. There are many versions of the egg contents. Here are some to get you started:[1]

- A plastic donkey for Jesus' entry into Jerusalem on Palm Sunday
- A piece of bread for the Last Supper
- Three dimes for the silver pieces given to Judas
- A nail for the nailing of Jesus to the cross
- A piece of fabric for the robe Jesus wore
- A small cross made of wood
- A piece of thorny flower stem for the crown of thorns
- A die for the casting of lots for his robe
- A rock for the tomb door
- A piece of gauze for the body wrappings
- Some whole cloves and cinnamon sticks for the spices that were brought to anoint the body
- A torn piece of cloth for the temple curtain that was torn

Discussing the origins of the Easter symbols is a fun activity.

There are many ideas about where these traditions got started. Look up these ideas at the library: the egg symbolizes new life that both spring and the Resurrection give, the lily represents new life, the bunny symbolizes new life and spring, and the lamb symbolizes new life and meekness. An interesting tidbit of information that we learned is that giving eggs on Easter got started because eggs weren't allowed during Lent at one time, so they celebrated the end of Lent by giving and eating eggs.

Some other ideas that we enjoy are:

- Making Easter crafts: caterpillars from egg cartons, bird nests, paper chains, etc.
- Watching a movie together: *The Greatest Story Ever Told, The Robe, Jesus of Nazareth,* etc.
- Read some Easter stories together: some books are suggested at the end of the chapter.
- Study how other countries celebrate Easter.
- Attend a sunrise service on Easter morning.
- Take a nature walk and discuss the analogies that spring has with Christ's life.
- Write thank-you notes to those who have been helpful in bringing love and hope into your life.

Decorating

To help show the reason for Easter and decorate your home at the same time, create a display on a table near the entryway of your home. Have on it some symbols of Easter: a cross, a crown of thorns, a large nail, and/or a purple sash (hang it on the cross if desired). One family I know changes the scarf from purple to black on Good Friday, then from black to white on Easter morning.

Another project my children enjoy is to create a Jesse tree with the names of Jesus on it. We take a small tree branch and a flowerpot and spray-paint them gold. Then we place some foam in the center of the pot and place the branch in the center of the foam. We then cut hearts (about three inches wide) out of construction paper, write a name on each, punch a hole in the top of the heart, and tie a ribbon loop through it. Each day from Ash Wednesday to Easter we place one name on the tree. This tree can also be placed on the entryway table with other Easter items.

$\mathcal{V}$ALENTINE'S DAY

We enjoy this holiday both as a family and as a special day for my husband and me. When I was young I thought this day should be a national holiday! It doesn't have to cost much to make it fun or romantic. It can be a special day to add to the family's memory bank, while costing pennies.

Decorating

A few simple touches can make this day special. Have the kids cut out paper hearts and decorate the house. Use different colors and types of paper (foil, lace, etc.). Make paper chains from red and white paper. Make a chain or wreath from valentines that you have received. We have found some great unopened Valentine's Day decorations at thrift stores too.

Making Memories

One of the things we do is study the origins of this day. We read about the saint called Valentine and why showing love is a feature of this day. You'll find several books in the library about this story.

Another one of my favorite things to do is to have my valentines remailed from America's Sweetheart City—Loveland, Colorado. For fifty-six years, Loveland has been offering its annual valentine's program to the public for free. Anyone can receive a unique stamp cancellation by placing the valentine that is to be mailed from Loveland in a stamped and addressed envelope, then inside a second envelope stamped and addressed to: Postmaster, ATTN: Valentines, USPS, Loveland, CO 80538-9998. Your valentine will be removed from the outer envelope and hand stamped with the Loveland cachet. To ensure that your valentine arrives by February 14, Loveland must receive it by February 3.

For your spouse, a touching gesture or gift will mean more than an expensive gift. Try some of these ideas:

- A nicely written list of all the reasons that you love and appreciate him or her. Go an extra step and *make* the paper that you write it on (see *Miserly Moms* for an easy recipe for making paper).
- Serve your loved one breakfast in bed.
- Cut out paper hearts and write love notes on them. Place them throughout the house (and in his or her lunch box) so he or she will find them all day.
- Put a heart-shaped cookie in his or her lunch.
- Go for a walk, holding hands.
- Make a coupon book filled with ways to say "I love you" (a back rub, a foot rub, doing his or her chores for a day, etc.).
- Pull out your wedding album and look through it together.
- Listen to romantic music (classical, Tony Bennett, Frank Sinatra).
- Send an e-mail to each other letting the other know he or she is being thought about.

We also try to make this a special day for the entire family. Here are a few other ideas that we do to make it special:

- Have the kids make a box to store valentines in: take an empty Kleenex box and cover it with decorative paper (wrapping paper, contact paper, colored tissue paper, etc.).
- Talk as a family about giving an extra gift to a missionary or a local organization that helps the poor. Go together and give the money (if possible), accompanied by a valentine that you made together.
- Make heart-shaped cookies with the kids. Decorate them with red or pink icing.
- Make chocolate heart Popsicles: get an inexpensive chocolate mold and sticks from a craft store and pour melted chocolate into the molds. Before they harden insert the sticks.
- Make strawberry milkshakes (and any other pink food you can think of).
- Make festive ice cubes: place candy hearts in ice-cube trays, fill with water, and freeze. Serve at dinner in the drinks.
- Study old-fashioned valentines and make one using doilies and construction paper.
- Bake a heart-shaped cake for the family dessert. Hide

cinnamon candy hearts throughout the cake!

- Make valentine placemats and cover them with clear contact paper.
- Make coupon books for one another.
- Make bookmarks for one another. Glue paper hearts to construction paper and decorate them with markers or rubber-stamping. Cover in contact paper to preserve.
- Have a candy treasure hunt.
- Do a science project: cut the base of the stem on a white carnation and put it in a glass of water that has red food coloring in it. In a few hours the flower will turn pink.
- Make an acrostic poem for someone with a valentine word: love, pink, red, heart, kiss, etc. Make each line something you like about that person.
- Watch a Charlie Brown movie together.

RESOURCES

Carlson, Melody. *Benjamin's Box.* Zondervan, 2000.

Colson, Chuck, Billy Graham, Max Lucado. *Christ in Easter, a Family Celebration of Holy Week.* NavPress, 1990.

Fisher, Diana. *Disney's Make Your Own Valentines.* Walter Foster, 1999.

Hibbard, Ann. *Family Celebrations at Easter.* Baker Book House, 1994.

Jackson, Dave, and Neta Jackson. *The Mayflower Secret.* Bethany House, 1998.

Kennedy, Pamela. *An Easter Celebration: Traditions and Customs From Around the World.* Ideals Children's Books, 1991.

McGovern, Ann. *The Pilgrim's First Thanksgiving.* Econo-Clad, 1998.

Ross, Kathy. *Best Holiday Crafts Ever.* Millbrook, 1996.

———. *Crafts for All Seasons.* Millbrook, 2000.

Russo, Steve. *Why Celebrate Easter.* Broadman Holman, 2001.

Scarlata, Robin. *A Family Guide to Biblical Holidays.* Heart of Wisdom Publishing, 2001.

Schmidt, Gary. *William Bradford: Plymouth's Faithful Pilgrim.* Eerdman's, 1998.

Talkington, Bruce. *Winnie the Pooh's Valentine Kit.* Disney Press, 1998.

"Thanksliving Box," by FamilyLife Today (that's not a typo!), *www.familylife.com.*

Waters, Kate. *Samuel Eaton's Day: A Day in the Life of a Pilgrim Boy.* Scholastic, 1996.

———. *Sarah Morton's Day: A Day in the Life of a Pilgrim Girl.* Scholastic, 1993.

Zimmerman, Martha. *Celebrating the Christian Year.* Bethany House, 1993.

CHAPTER FIVE

Decorating and Furnishing Your Home

The only really good place to buy lumber is at a store where the lumber has already been cut and attached together in the form of furniture.

—Dave Barry, *The Taming of the Screw*

$ $ $

*A*s with holiday decorating and celebrations, I believe we can have a beautiful home and still be frugal. The miserly home does not mean orange crates and broken furniture. With a bit of creativity, we can have attractive homes that welcome our guests. I hope some of these ideas from our home will help you to show your style in your home.

DECORATING

Plan

Planning is the key to making any change worth its time and expense. But you don't have to be a decorator to plan well! To get started, take a look at several magazines on decorating. You'll find magazines with overall decorating ideas as well as those that specialize in walls and windows, kitchens, children's rooms, etc. Take a look at how they do certain rooms and get a feel for what you like.

Once you know what your goal is, be realistic. Your room will never look like that picture-perfect room in the magazine, but it can still look great! The magazines are good for pointing us in the right direction as to style, arrangement of the room, and color schemes.

Next, get a good grasp on what your family's needs are. They may not appreciate (or be able to use) an Americana living room that can't be played in. They may need a comfortable, livable place that pleases the eye as well. This can be done!

The DON'TS of Redecorating

Don't throw away old, rusty, or torn furniture: repaint or recover as often as possible.

Don't clutter: it's hard to clean and it overwhelms the eye! Store as many things as possible and rotate them into the room.

Don't think everything has to match. Use complementary colors.

Don't buy new: scour thrift stores, flea markets, and garage sales.

Where to Start

Don't throw out the sofa and other furniture! You can probably work with them. Maybe a change of other things in the room will make them work better. Wait until after you do the rest of the tips before you decide to replace them.

The key to any redecorating is to *simplify*. Decluttering your home will make quite a change in its appearance and will leave you more room to do other things. In order to declutter, we need to creatively make some storage space. Many of the "hiding" techniques can also be decorations that we add to the room. Here are some ideas to help you clean up and decorate:

- Hide the TV, VCR, and videos in an armoire or cabinet.
- Box up out-of-season items (winter coats, boots, blankets, sleds, for example) in plastic garbage cans that can be stored in the garage, basement, or storage shed. They are about $10 apiece and can hold many things.
- Store out-of-season clothes and blankets in pillow shams, and use them as decoration on guest beds, couches, etc.
- Store extra board games under a sofa that has a skirt to hide them.

- Use suitcases to store extra pillows, blankets, sweaters, etc.
- Use a wooden storage trunk as a coffee table: ours holds wrapping paper and ribbon.
- My grandmother's coffee table was a large round table with four legs. She draped a floor-length cloth over it and used the space under the table for storage. No one knew!
- Cover cardboard boxes with colorful contact paper and store children's toys in them.

What's Most Important

Once you've cleaned out the clutter, you want to get down to the real decorating. But you have very little money. Where do you start? Decorators have an order that they follow. The areas listed below are in the order that we should consider change. They are what we see first and what most affects the way we feel about a room.

The Floors

The floor creates the style of a room. If the floor is "off" from the rest of the room, the entire room will be off. Changing a sofa or table isn't going to make that incongruence go away. If it's a different color or theme than the room, fix it. And it isn't as hard as it seems! If tearing up the floor isn't possible, then consider some of these simpler ways to fix the flooring:

- Repaint the linoleum. This is a realistic option if it is in good shape but the wrong color. Be creative and make a pattern on the floor: stencil, using a pattern that matches the room (leaves or lace doilies, for example), make bold checks in two complementary colors, paint cobblestones, paint bricks, etc.
- Add throw rugs in the colors of the room.
- Lay a fitted wall-to-wall rug over the carpet (this is cheaper than re-carpeting).

The Walls

The next thing that our eyes are naturally drawn to are the walls. This involves both color and how we decorate them. First, pick a color that works with the furniture in the room. But also remember that color sets the mood. Choose something that you want the room to reflect. I have a lavender room that is peaceful, and I have a room with one bright orange wall that gives energy but is not overpowering (since it's only one wall).

A great way to repaint rooms in designer paints and colors at a low cost is to visit your local hardware store. Often custom paints are mixed in the wrong shade. The customer who ordered them cannot use them and they are often sold at a very low price. There is nothing wrong with the paint and it is usually of a high-grade quality. If you can be flexible on the color, this is a great find.

How Much Paint?

To accurately calculate the amount of paint you will need, measure the perimeter of the room and the height of the walls. Multiply the perimeter by the height of one wall and it will give you the square footage of that room. Or, for the math challenged, plan on one gallon of paint covering around 300 square feet of wall.

If you like the color of your room but it is faded or marked up, try sponging an alternate color on the wall. The alternate color could be picked up from a piece of furniture that you want to keep in the room but the color isn't quite right. Sponging can blend that color in as well as perk up the walls. Another way to add other colors is to use wallpaper borders. A border can contain the main wall color as well as the complementary color that you want to add. Borders are inexpensive and easy to apply.

Another idea for improving the look of a room is to wallpaper. This is more costly and time consuming than paint but can add a classy touch. Of course, papering one wall can improve a room and cost much less than papering the entire room. Wallpaper can be purchased at 50 percent off from mail order companies. Check the back pages of magazines for ads that offer these savings.

After you complete the painting/papering, arrange wall hangings so they are pleasing to the eye. Group them together or place larger single pieces on each wall. Do theme groupings, such as family photos together or similar prints. Experiment to get a feel for how groupings affect the room. Also when hanging pictures, sit down on the sofa or chair to get a true eye for where they should be hung. We tend to hang them too high because we do it while standing. Most people are sitting in the room when they look at pictures on the walls.

Be creative with frames for pictures or mirrors. I used old barn wood to frame a painting and a mirror in one room. It gives the room a rustic feel. Find old frames at thrift stores and repaint them.

The Windows

How do the curtains fit the theme of the room? Replacing curtains is costly, but we can still change their impression while working with what we have. If the quality of the curtain is good but not the right color or style, that can be fixed. By adding something to the curtains, you can blend them into the room. Try rubberstamping or stenciling a design that will match the theme and color of a room onto plain curtains. Another idea is to sew trim along the edges and bottom of curtains in a fabric type and color that coordinates. If the curtain fabric is old and needs to be replaced, there are still some cheap options. First, look at thrift stores for new curtains. If that doesn't work, check with decorators who may have removed some good curtains from a customer's home. Many bed and linen stores sell designer sheets for 50 percent off when a season changes or a designer's line changes. These make great decorator tools. I covered an existing curtain with a designer sheet in a pattern and color that matched our room. I laid the old curtain flat and spread the designer sheet over it. Then I turned the edges of the sheet over the edge of the curtain, hemmed all four edges, and rehung it. It gave the room a face-lift at very little cost.

The Lighting

Lighting sets the mood of a room. If you have harsh fluorescent overhead lighting, the room will feel cold and impersonal. Softer lighting coming from lamps or track lighting makes a room feel warm and inviting. The best lighting of all is natural lighting! Uncover those windows and let the light in. If you don't want to see the view from your windows, use a sheer or lace curtain to block the view but still allow the light in.

Tips

We can do many little things to improve a room's feel. Here are a few of my favorites:

- Buy used lamps at thrift stores and recover the lampshades with fabric that complements your room. If you like the shape of the base of the lamp, it can also be repainted or decoupaged to match the room.
- Replace the curtain rod with something that fits the theme of your room: a rustic-looking tree branch, a thick grapevine, a fishing pole, a canoe oar, a pool cue, a bamboo pole, etc.
- Add new pillows to a sofa. Use colors from other items in the room to tie the room together.
- Buy a small round decorator table (sold at most Kmart and Target stores for under $5) and cover with a cloth that ties in a color from something else in the room. Use a tablecloth or designer sheet.
- A simple tablecloth can brighten up a room or change its mood. But we don't need to buy one for every change we want to make. Using attractive bed sheets works very well. Pick a sheet with a pattern that you like, and you're done! No hemming needed!
- Add a wicker basket to the room, and use it to store magazines, shoes, toys, etc., that would otherwise clutter the floor.
- Use a folding screen to divide a room.
- Add plants to liven things up.

Thrift stores can be filled with treasures if you know how to look. In order to find the best goods, visit the thrift shops frequently. Their products turn over often as new merchandise is donated and the older items are sold. Find out which days donations are taken. Shop those days to get the best items.

Furnishing

Furnishing a home can be very expensive. In addition to the big-ticket items such as sofas and tables, there are lamps and end tables, headboards and footboards, and so much more. But making a home look homey and warm doesn't have to cost a fortune or require a second income. With a little resourcefulness and creativity, a small amount of cash can go a long way.

We know firsthand what it's like to start from scratch. When Beau and I were first married, we rented rooms in furnished homes. When we found our own place, it was not furnished. For a bed, we spread the sheet out on the floor at night. Friends lent us their foam camping pad until we saved enough for a mattress. For a table, we borrowed a rickety card table from a friend and some metal folding chairs from the church. If we cut anything firmly on it, the table wobbled. One person had to hold the table while the other cut. For the television stand, we covered an old trunk with a cloth. We eventually furnished the apartment from our savings and by looking for store sales (the mattress), garage sales (the dining table), and asking our families if they had furniture they weren't using (my mom's old couch). Hard work, creativity, and resourcefulness pay off.

Where to Buy

Consider many places to buy home furnishings, including department stores and furniture stores, estates sales, and thrift shops. Some families go even further and make their furniture themselves. We have done each of these things at one time or another throughout our marriage. Let's walk through each type of purchase.

Department Stores and Furniture Stores

Department stores and furniture stores can be great places to buy furniture if you know what you are looking for and how to buy. Knowing what you need and want is the most important step. Do you need a loveseat or a full-size couch, a dining table that seats six to eight or a small kitchen table? What are the measurements for the space each piece will live in? If you don't know exactly what you need, you will end up buying more than necessary or even the wrong item.

Once you have a shopping list, start watching for sales. Many sale items are great deals. Many are not. To know if you have a good deal or not, figure what the store's profit is. A furniture store makes $55 on every $100 of the full retail price. So the sale price should be at least 50 percent off of retail to be a good price.

Whatever you buy, make sure that the furniture is manufactured well (see "Tips for Buying Furniture" on page 70). If buying new, make sure there is a warranty against manufacturing defects (such as broken internal frames, tearing fabric, excessively wearing fabric, etc.). Also try to get delivery included. That will save you a backache.

Direct From Manufacturers

By obtaining a business license and resale number from your city, you can buy furnishings directly from manufacturers at a great discount. You can also make arrangements directly with custom laborers, cutting out the middleman. However, this option may not be profitable for you if you will only be buying a few pieces of furniture.

Outlet Stores

Some furniture outlet stores cater to the public. These are no-frills warehouses that have a few samples on display and you order from these. For people who live in smaller cities, this is a great way to get a lower price. These places are good sources for large furniture items as long as you can get the warranty and check the quality of the construction on the demo models.

Mail Order

Other outlet centers are available to anyone in the USA—by mail. They offer name-brand furniture at up to 50 percent off retail. These folks have the goods but don't have expensive overhead, so they sell direct to you for less. Shipping the furniture adds very little to the overall price. In order to buy from them, have the manufacturer's name, model number, size, and any other details you need (color, type of finish on the wood). Here are a few of these stores:

- Cedar Rack Furniture
  Box 515
  Hudson, NC 28638
  (704) 396-2361

- Quality Furniture Market
  2034 Hickory Blvd. SW
  Lenoir, NC 28645
  (828) 728-2964
- Blackwelders' Industries (carries various manufacturers and minimal fee for catalogs)
  Route 18, Box 8
  Stateville, NC 28677
  (800) 438-0201
  http://blackwelders.homefurnishing.com
- Furniture Choices
  2501 Peters Creek Parkway
  Winston Salem, NC 27107
  (336) 720-9700
  www.furniturechoices.com
- Designer Secrets
  P.O. Box 529
  Fremont, NE 68025
  (800) 955-2559

Many of the furniture manufacturers are located in North Carolina. One place that they congregate is called the Hickory Furniture Mart. There are hundreds of retailers plus a few manufacturers represented. To get a listing of all of them, call their general number (800-462-MART) or write them at:

- Hickory Furniture Mart
  2220 Highway 70 SE
  Hickory, NC 28602

If you would like a comprehensive list of furniture mail-order companies, buy (or check the library) *The Wholesale-by-Mail Catalog* (HarperCollins).

Garage Sales

Other treasure hunts are garage sales. These can harbor gold mines or garbage dumps. Some ways to assure that you find gold are:

- Shop early. Later in the day means less selection.

- Be fair in your offers. Here are some guidelines:

    Housewares and clothing items should be around ¹⁄₁₀ of their retail value.

    Larger items such as furniture or appliances should be ¼ of their retail value.

- Make a list of the sales you want to visit. Plan them out on a map.
- Search behind items, since others may be hiding.
- Check carefully for damage—pick up the item and scan all surfaces. Ask to plug it in and operate it if it is electrical.
- Barter—think of the maximum that you will pay and offer a bit less to start.

Numerous families successfully furnish their homes with quality products found at garage sales—and they all have great stories to go with their finds. I have seen people sell excellent items for pennies on the dollar: dressers bought for $10, designer dishes for $5 a set, headboard with mattress and box springs for $20. We found a solid maple dining table with six chairs for $75. We still have it today (twenty years later)! Families who have furnished their homes with these treasures have been featured in newspapers and books. Their homes are lovely, not cheap looking. With a little determination, you can have a lovely home on a shoestring.

Tips for Buying Furniture

Buying furniture that is made from wood requires that you make sure it is solid wood. Check the top of the piece first. Ask if the wood is veneer (a thin layer of real wood attached to particle board or cheap wood). If it is, avoid it. Veneer can chip easily. If the item is made from solid wood, the finish can be restored, so don't be put off by marks. Small scratches can be covered with stain or wax. Water marks can be removed from solid wood by stripping the finish and applying oxalic acid, then refinishing. Deep gouges or burns, however, are more difficult. These may require filling the gouge or bleaching the stain, and it may be noticeable later.

Once you have checked the quality of the wood and its finish, check the quality of the construction. For tables, the legs should be stable and not wobble, and the corners should be glued and screwed into place. We bought some wooden chairs at a garage sale that had joints that were glued but not screwed. We constantly had to deal with breaking and re-gluing parts.

For cabinets and dressers, joints should be dovetailed (interlocking wood) and not just nailed. Legs should not be screwed in this case. Screws should join any hardware such as handles or knobs. Drawers should have guides and stops.

Sofas are only as good as the frame they are constructed around. Find out, if you can, what type of wood it was made of and how the frame was built. Soft woods, such as pine, will break sooner. Also try to find out what types of spring and foam were used. Certain types of foam break down quickly, creating a sinking effect when you sit down. The cheaper the foam, the sooner it will break down. Poor quality cushion foam can be replaced with high-density foam and wrapped in polyester fiber before covering it. You should be able to exert pressure on the arms of a chair and not feel any give. Feel for springs in the cushions and check the underside of the piece for them.

Sofa bed mattresses come in two types: solid foam and innerspring. Solid foam means it has no springs but is made of filling and padding: large slabs of foam are covered by a mattress pad. These are good for sofa beds that won't be used a great deal. Foam mattresses break down quickly. Innerspring mattresses have coils in them. Better quality mattresses will have lots of springs. A good mattress will quickly return to its original shape after you get up. The edges should not be worn at all, and you should not be able to feel the coils when you press down on the mattress.

Reuse What You Have

Before you throw something out or go looking to purchase something, think of what you can do with what you have, such as recover an old sofa. If you have a fine sofa but the material is worn or stained, find fabric that you like and recover it. For this, you can use a nice sheet or buy a heavier fabric at an upholstery fabric outlet store. They have the ends of the fabric rolls that furniture stores used. Remove the old fabric in sections with a razor edge and use them as the pattern (add two inches to each side for tucking and mistakes). Attach the fabric to the existing seams with a staple gun. Our loveseat cost me $60 to recover myself. I was quoted $500 to have it done by someone else.

Try these creative reuse and decorating tips:

- Make a bed ruffle with three-to-four yards of fabric and attach to an old sheet.
- Decorate walls with stenciling.
- Pretty tablecloths can be draped as swags over windows.
- Make a mirror out of an old picture frame.
- Make tables or benches out of old doors.
- Fill antique shoes with dried flowers.
- Use an old small wheelbarrow as a magazine rack.
- Use an old jug for the base of a lamp.
- Use a colorful blanket or quilt for a curtain.
- Recover the cushions on your sofa or throw pillows.
- Perk up a tired lamp with lace or notions.
- Brighten a curtain rod with gold or silver spray paint.
- Add a mirror to a small room to make it seem larger.
- Use old clothing to make something new:
  throw pillows
  quilts
  basket liners
  dishtowels
  braided rugs (wool)
  placemats
  coasters
  drapes
  guest towels

RESOURCES

Barnes, Emilie. *Decorating Dreams on a Budget*. Harvest House, 1999.

Causey, Kimberly. *The Insider's Guide to Buying Home Furnishings— How and Where Anyone Can Buy High-Quality Designer Brands at Wholesale Prices Without Hiring a Designer*. Home Decor Press, 1996.

Stewart Wray, Jo. *The Cheapskate's Guide to Home Decorating.* Citadel Press, 2000.

Tolley, Emelie. *Flea Market Style: Decorating With a Creative Edge.* Potter, 1998.

CHAPTER SIX

Fun in the Sun: Vacations

I'm sorry, ma'am, but I'm afraid your husband doesn't qualify as a carry-on item.

—McPherson cartoon

$ $ $

*Y*ou and your spouse have slaved away for a long time without a break and you need a vacation. You're ready to head to the beach or mountains or desert (or all three, if you live in California).

The first thing you may want to ask yourself is, *Why am I taking a vacation?* There may be any number of reasons. The most obvious is to get away from work and recharge your batteries: perhaps relax with a good book, soak up some rays, or do a little body surfing or Boogie boarding.

Vacations can also be a wonderful time of family bonding. Just hanging out with one another without the pressures of jobs, schoolwork, housework, lawn work, cooking, laundry, and lots of other chores can reveal new or previously unknown personality quirks, traits, and characteristics.

A vacation can also be a time for exploring areas of the country that you've never visited before. Many people from the East or Midwest, for example, are astounded by the beauty and grandeur of the American West.

In any case, vacations are meant to be times of refreshment and relaxation. But how often have we experienced just the opposite? Chevy Chase practically made a career out of the holidays-gone-awry theme with his various vacation movies.

ℕECESSITY OF PLANNING

The single most important aspect to having a successful vacation is planning. Without careful planning, a vacation can turn into a living nightmare. Murphy's Law—whatever can go wrong, will—seems to be especially operative when it comes to vacations. A carefully planned vacation doesn't mean, however, that there isn't any room for spur-of-the-moment activities. A side trip to the Painted Desert or St. Augustine or a Civil War battle site can sometimes prove to be the highlight of an entire vacation. It just means that these unplanned excursions need to occur within an already carefully worked out plan.

Planning is essential to any type of vacation, whether it's a simple weekend spent in a tent or a month traveling throughout the Southwest. In some ways, the simpler—or perhaps, the more frugal—the vacation, the more planning is needed. For example, tent camping is one of the most economical vacations but can require the most planning. There are hundreds of details that need to be taken care of.

Some of those pesky details to consider are:

- How will you get to your destination? If you are flying, where will you leave your car?
- Where will you eat along the way? Will you take a cooler for most meals and save the restaurant expense?
- How much will you pack? Pack less clothing than you need—there are Laundromats along the way.
- Will you look for a motel with a kitchen so you can save on restaurant meals?
- Have you made a list of items to bring so nothing gets left out? Some travel books have starter lists that you can add to.

How Long to Stay?

An important consideration when planning a vacation is to think about how long you want to stay. A vacation can be anything from a weekend to months. Typically it is one or two weeks in the summer. American companies are usually less generous with vacation time than their European counterparts, which often give workers a month or more off.

Many families have found that three weeks is just about ideal for a family summer vacation. You spend the first week adjusting to the fact that you are in a different place with a different routine. The second week is generally the high point. You've acquired the vacation mindset, your burn is turning to a tan, and you don't have a care in the world. Sometime during the third week the reality that your vacation is about to end starts to set in. The tendency here, which should be resisted, is to try to squeeze every single last bit of enjoyment out of the remaining days. This is usually a formula for frustration and despair. Better just to sit back, relax, and let the remaining days go by with as little thought as possible to their ending.

Most of us, however, can only take one week for a vacation. When we had zero money, we spent our vacation camping. For a few dollars a night, we could enjoy the outdoors and go hiking, swimming, or fishing. We drove up the coast of California and visited the beauty of northern California—a different spot each day. One word of caution: we found a week of camping to be too long. We tired of the uncomfortable beds, dirt in our clothes, and poor clean-up facilities. Make sure you can handle that much "roughing it" before you plan on it for more than a couple of days.

Before You Leave . . .

- Have your mail and newspaper picked up daily by a neighbor or friend (having it stopped alerts people to the fact that you are gone).
- Have a neighbor watch for parcels or packages that may be left at your door.
- Leave a phone number with a friend or neighbor where you can be reached in case of emergency.
- Turn off your water heater and turn down (or off) the furnace or air-conditioner thermostat.
- Put any perishables in the freezer instead of leaving them in the refrigerator.

Minivacations can also be very refreshing. This could be

anything from a night downtown to a three-day weekend. Many hotels and resorts offer special prices for these mini-stays, and you can often get special airfares if you have a flexible schedule or can leave at the drop of a hat. I know families that take several three-day weekends throughout the year instead of one long vacation.

*T*YPES OF VACATIONS

What pops into your mind when you think of a vacation? If you've been watching any TV, it's probably a romantic getaway to a secluded South Sea island or a cruise through the Caribbean. These are, of course, classic images of vacations. But for the frugal family, a vacation of this type is probably not a reality: they're just too expensive.

However, lots of really relaxing and fun vacations couples and families can enjoy don't put a major crimp in the budget. These include: tent camping, staying in a cabin, borrowing or renting a motor home, renting a vacation home, exchanging a home with someone in another part of the country or in a foreign country, vacation packages, vacationing during the off-season, and even traditional motel vacationing.

When picking the type of vacation to have with children, it will go smoother if you keep a few tips in mind. First, plan the trip with your kids, but not around your kids. Their interests should be considered in the planning, but don't let them dictate what type of trip you will take. Involve them in the planning and go over brochures and pictures with them. Second, even though you will plan most of the vacation, allow for spontaneous side trips that appeal more to the kids than to you. Third, avoid long bus or car rides. If you need to travel for a long period, take breaks. Fourth, allow for downtime or playtime each day. Fifth, make sure snacks and rest stops are fitted into the daily schedule. Sixth, with children of different ages and interests, occasionally divide up into smaller groups and see different things.

Tent Camping

Let's face it. Not everyone likes to camp. But it yields some wonderful family expeditions and a wonderful experience of the great outdoors.

One of the greatest pleasures of camping is experiencing nature up close and personal. Few things are more exhilarating than coming out of a tent on a crisp summer morning to behold one of the incredible vistas that you often encounter when camping. And there's nothing quite like a meal cooked over a campfire after a long day of hiking or fishing.

Another thing to remember is that, somewhat perversely, there seems to be an inverse relationship between the beauty of the campsite and the quality of the hygiene facilities. We have found that invariably the best campgrounds are equipped with what are euphemistically called "vault facilities," which are nothing more than a hole in the ground with some kind of structure over it (these used to be called outhouses). If you can tolerate doing your business in one of these facilities, you're a better person than I.

Some of the best campsites can be found in the National Forest Service system. These camps typically are the most beautiful, least expensive—and most primitive. Don't expect hot showers and fancy plumbing. Some even lack running water. Often the more uncivilized campground has the more sensational view. There are also many beautiful private, state, and national park campgrounds, although the private ones tend to be more expensive and the parks more crowded.

Planning—the Key to Successful Camping

While planning is necessary for any vacation, it is absolutely essential for camping. The first thing to decide is where to camp. I enjoy camping out West. I know that there are many lovely places to camp in other regions, but since most of my experience comes from camping in the West, let me explain why I like it so much. A number of factors contribute to this; among them are the scenery, weather, availability, and diversity of campgrounds.

It's almost as if the West was specially created to be camped in. Perhaps most notable is the spectacular scenery. The mountains of Colorado, the national parks of southern Utah, the desert Southwest, the redwoods and beaches of California—all provide breathtaking vistas. The sights, the sounds, and the smells are often amazing. There's nothing quite like waking up in a pine forest, or hiking through the desert in springtime, or the gentle murmur of surf and the tangy salt smell of the ocean.

The weather out West is also ideal for camping. I don't know about you, but for me there's nothing worse than trying to sleep outside when it's 85 degrees and 95 percent humidity. Typically, especially at any elevation, summer in the West will feature bright, sunshiny days and cool, crisp nights ideal for sleeping. Some parts of the West experience a monsoonlike season in late summer and early fall, but that usually means possible short bursts of showers and thunderstorms in the late afternoon followed by evening clearing and crystalline nights. If you do camp out West, you'll want to be prepared for nighttime temperatures that can get as low as the upper thirties, even in the summer.

Check your library or bookstore for books that list and describe the features of campgrounds. You'll want a book that tells you the relative beauty of the setting, number and size of actual campsites, special features about particular sites, proximity to adjacent campsites (how close do you want your tent to someone else's?), access to the campground (easy or difficult), facilities, nearby activities, quality of hiking trails, availability of fishing/hunting, and how to reserve a site. You will want to be sure you know what the reservation policies are well in advance of when you actually plan to be there. Some of the more popular campgrounds fill up months ahead of actual occupancy. Two of my favorite travel books that offer all of these services are *Family Travel* and *Free Vacations and Bargain Adventures in the USA*—both by Evelyn Kaye. Other travel books are listed in the resource section at the end of the chapter.

Before venturing out with the tent, make sure that you are prepared. It will help make the trip more enjoyable. Following are some essential items to plan for (for a more thorough listing, check a camping guidebook):

- Insects (bring bug repellant)
- Adequate padding under your sleeping bag (test it out by sleeping on it before leaving)
- Rain gear for surprise cloudbursts
- Skill in putting up and tearing down the tent (practice in the backyard)
- System for protecting your food and gear from curious ani-

mals (keeping it locked in the car is helpful)
- Readiness for ripe fragrances that waft from bodies unwashed for days on end

Our experience is that something special often happens when we tent camp. Few of us have the opportunity to experience the beauty of creation on a regular basis. Getting away from life in the city or suburbs—or even a small town—and out into nature can be tremendously restorative.

Motor Home Camping

Another way to have a relatively inexpensive vacation is to borrow or rent a friend's motor home. This, of course, presupposes (a) that you have friends, (b) that at least one of them has a motor home, and (c) that they'll let you use it. Having never vacationed this way, I can't give you firsthand knowledge about all the protocol associated with actually obtaining a borrowed motor home. I have heard that this usually comes about as a result of the friend's telling a select circle of friends that such a vehicle is available for their use. In other words, the friend initiates the conversation about the availability of his motor home, not you.

If you do indeed obtain use of such a vehicle, remember that motor home camping is quite different from tent camping. For example, the number of available campgrounds is smaller as well as the number of motor home sites within campgrounds. You are also one step removed from nature (which can be good or bad). The vehicle itself will guzzle gas like you won't believe. You can't make as good time on the road. You will find yourself transformed into the guy everyone hates who has traffic backed up for miles as you struggle to make it up the mountain on that two-lane road.

Nevertheless, you'll find plenty of spectacular motor home camping opportunities, and the people who take these vacations often swear by them. They offer the convenience of not having to pack and unpack, you are more protected from the weather, and you can cook in a real kitchen.

Renting a Vacation Home

Believe it or not, renting a vacation home can be quite reasonable. We know a family of eight that has gone back to the same vacation area on the East Coast for nearly twenty years. Each year they have rented a beach house, and (as this is being written) are still able to get one for under $500 a week. If you look hard enough, you can find bargains. If you are interested in a specific city, check out the phone book for that city at your local library. You can also call the Chamber of Commerce in that city and ask for a listing of all vacation rentals in the area.

Staying With Relatives or Friends

One time-tested way to cut down on vacation costs is to stay at the home of friends or relatives. If you live in Illinois and have relatives or friends who live in Colorado, perhaps they will invite you to visit them. This can make for a pleasant enough vacation, provided several things are in place.

First, have they really made it clear that you're welcome? Sometimes people will offer to have you visit them not really expecting you to take them up on it. If they offer, check it out with them. Ask them if they're sure it's okay, and be sure to plan in advance when you'll be there so they have time to get things ready for you.

Second, don't stay too long. Remember, fish and relatives begin to stink after a few days. It's probably better to have a stay at a friend or relative's house be part of a larger vacation plan, where you spend, say, only three days out of two weeks there. An extended visit by a large gang of people can place a tremendous burden on a family.

Third, be genuinely grateful for the opportunity to stay there, and find a way to express your gratitude beyond a thank-you note (which you should always send). One way is to offer to take them out to dinner. Or perhaps you could offer to pay for an excursion to a nearby national park or monument.

Motel Vacations

It is not out of the question for families to plan reasonably priced vacations and stay in motels. Once again, the key is planning in advance. If you book rooms far enough ahead, you can sometimes save 10 to 20 percent even in season. You'll want to do some shopping around at the library or a bookstore: get the best travel guide for your vacation area; copy down names and numbers of places to stay that look interesting; call, write, or e-mail them for a brochure; and then do a little comparison pricing. Brochures can be very helpful because they not only give you complete descriptions of facilities but also give you full-color pictures of the motel, its rooms, lounges, and the surroundings. Sometimes this can be misleading, but when combined with guidebook recommendations, it generally pays off.

When thinking about a motel vacation, it is a good idea to think about a motel as a headquarters. For example, you might want to think about getting a motel in Durango, Colorado, or Moab, Utah, as a headquarters, or base, for exploring the high desert, Four Corners area, or southern Utah. Santa Fe would make a good base for the New Mexico highlands, and Sedona, Arizona, for the desert Southwest. And northern Arkansas would be an ideal spot for touring the Ozarks, Missouri, and the beauty there. Or you could just stay put in any one of these places. All of them have lots to do. To be even more frugal, find a motel in a less touristy town near your primary destination; it's sometimes cheaper. For example, rent a motel in Cortez, Colorado, rather than Durango to visit the Four Corners.

To get the best discount on a room, make sure you are talking with a supervisor or hotel manager. They are the ones who can make pricing decisions. If you are using the toll-free number for a chain hotel, call the individual hotel directly to see if they can do any better. Sometimes they are hungry for business and will offer better prices. Also use any travel club discounts that you might have (such as AAA—American Automobile Association or AARP—American Association of Retired Persons).

The day of the week can also affect the price you pay. Some more popular spots will be busier on the weekends and may offer lower midweek rates. The same goes for in-season and off-season periods. Some off-season periods are just fine, weather wise, and are less crowded.

Other Vacation Housing Options

YMCA

The YMCA offers clean and affordable housing all over the nation. To see if one of their forty nationwide locations is near your destination, contact:

- The Y's Way
  224 E. 47th Street
  New York, NY 10017
  (212) 308-2899
  www.ymcanyc.org/reservations/yway.html

Hostels

Check out the youth hostels. They cost as little as $10 per night per person:

- American Youth Hostels
  733 15th Street, NW
  Suite 840
  Washington, D.C. 20005
  (202) 783-6161
  www.hiayh.org
- Elderhostels
  11 Avenue de Lafayette
  Boston, MA 02110-1746
  (877) 426-8056
  www.elderhostel.org

Swapping Homes

Another way to vacation at a very low price is to swap your home. Exchanging homes can save you the single highest cost of vacationing—the money you pay to stay somewhere. It can also save on food because it is much cheaper to do your own cooking than to eat out.

For those who are serious about house swapping, there are organizations that can help put you in touch with other house swappers. You pay an annual fee that ranges from $30–75 to list a description of your home on a Web site and/or in a catalog.

If one or several of the listings look interesting, you contact the people and provide details about your own home, its location, and possible swap dates. Potential house swappers will also be contacting you. It is good to start sending letters of inquiry at least six months in advance.

Details such as paying utilities, pet care, car use, and lawn care can all be negotiated. It is wise to put these agreements in writing. Though not legal documents, they can help avoid misunderstandings. The following are addresses for some of the home swapping services:

- HomeLink U.S.
  P.O. Box 650
  Key West, FL 33041
  (800) 628-3841
  www.homelink.org
  (the largest listing service)
  Cost: $50 to list your home on the Web site; more for the catalog
- Intervac
  30 Corte San Fernando
  Tiburon, CA 94920
  (800) 756-4663
  www.intervac.com
  Cost: $50 to list your home on the Web site
- International Home Exchange Network
  118 Flamingo Ave.
  Daytona Beach, FL 32118
  (386) 238-3633
  www.ihen.com
  Cost: $30 to list on the Web site
- Trading Home International
  P.O. Box 787
  Hermosa Beach, CA 90254
  (800) 877-TRADE
  trading-homes.com
  Cost: $65 to list on the Web site

- Home Exchange
  P.O. Box 30085
  Santa Barbara, CA 93130
  (866) 898-9660
  www.homeexchange.com
  Cost: $30 to list on the Web site

Homestays

Similar to house swapping, a homestay involves living in someone else's home. The major differences are (1) you actually stay with the host family, and (2) it always involves staying in a foreign country. The concept grew out of student exchange programs and has now been extended to families and other groups of adults.

The big appeal of homestays is that you can get a deeper understanding of a foreign culture by staying in someone's home than by staying in a motel. I have never actually experienced a homestay, but I nevertheless can think of some drawbacks: language difficulties, little or no privacy, few opportunities to just hang out and relax, plenty of opportunities for major cultural faux pas. But if you're adventurous, a homestay might be just the thing for you. Here are some addresses for homestay sources:

- American-International Homestays
  P.O. Box 1754
  Nederland, CO 80466
  (303) 258-3234
  www.aihtravel.com
  Services: Places travelers with English-speaking hosts in many countries
- AmeriSpan
  P.O. Box 40007
  Philadelphia, PA 19106-0007
  (800) 879-6640
  www.amerispan.com
  Services: Arranges language study and homestays at more than 35 schools in many Latin American countries
- Friendship Force
  34 Peachtree St.
  Suite 900

Atlanta, GA 30303
(404) 522-9490
www.friendship-force.org
- LEX America
  68 Leonard St.
  Suite 9
  Belmont, MA 02478-2566
  (617) 489-5800
  www.lexlrf.com
  Services: Arranges homestays for adults, families, and students in Japan and Korea. Also arranges opportunities for U.S. families to host foreign visitors.
- Servas
  11 John St.
  Room 505
  New York, NY 10038-4009
  (212) 267-0252
  http://servas.org
  Services: Produces a directory providing descriptions of homestay opportunities in many countries.
- World Learning (formerly Experiment in International Living)
  P.O. Box 676
  Brattleboro, VT 05302-0676
  (802) 257-7751
  www.worldlearning.org
  Services: Provides one- to four-week homestays in many countries

Vacation Clubs

Have you ever gotten a call from a "travel agent" offering you four days and three nights free in some semiexotic place like Myrtle Beach, Orlando, or Tucson? All you have to do is attend a short "presentation" and collect your free vacation. When you show up, the "presentation" turns out to be a hard-sell sales pitch to sign up for five, ten, or twenty years of vacations at special discounted prices. Yes, you can pick up your free vacation without buying anything, but not until you've been told in no uncertain terms you're an idiot if you don't sign up for one of the packages. If you end up not taking the bait, be prepared to be treated like a pariah, a scoundrel, and a fool.

The package deals themselves will save you money in the long run if you are already in the habit of taking fairly expensive vacations in places like the West Indies, Bermuda, or Cancun, and if you have a large chunk of change to plunk down. If you don't have the cash handy and have to finance the outlay (which will be thousands of dollars), you will probably end up losing. We have friends who have signed up for these packages who are satisfied that they've gotten a good deal, but they're not really in the same tax bracket as we are.

FLYING OR DRIVING

Okay. You know where you want to go, everyone's excited, but how do you get there? Drive or fly? Of course if you're going to Bermuda it's a little difficult to get there by car. But what if you're going from St. Louis to Santa Fe? You could easily drive it in two days (one, if you're a real road warrior). Or you could fly into Albuquerque, rent a car, and drive up there. Unless you are a travel agent (where you can save up to 75 percent), work for the airlines (where you can get free flights for you and your family), or have a gazillion frequent flyer miles saved up, driving will probably be a lot

---

Overseas Travel Tips

- Drink only bottled water with a seal that you must break in order to open (unless you are confident of that country's water quality). I specifically mention the lid because of an incident we had overseas. We asked for bottled water to be put in our rooms for teeth brushing and drinking. One afternoon we returned early and found the maid filling our bottled water containers from the tap!
- Drink only sodas that come in cans or bottles (no fountain sodas).
- Don't drink anything with ice in it.
- Don't rinse your toothbrush under the faucet—use your bottled water.
- Don't eat fresh vegetables or fruits (unless the skin is peeled off by you). The water used to wash them can be contaminated.
- Avoid raw or undercooked meats, shellfish, or fish.
- If you get "the crud," drink plenty of safe fluids.

cheaper, especially if you have a large family and they're all going.

A good way to save money if you're driving to your vacation is through coupon books. These are available for free at rest areas along major interstates. They usually contain discount coupons for food, lodging, and other travel expenses. Motels, looking to fill rooms that would otherwise go empty, offer substantial discounts off their regular rates. It is wise to call ahead and reserve the room, using the coupon. They'll advise right then if they are full. Usually there are at least two or three participating motels at each exit, so you should be able to find something to meet your family's needs. Another source of coupons is the Entertainment Books sold by schools and organizations as fund-raisers. These coupons are usually good nationwide. A friend of ours, who bought a Colorado Entertainment Book, paid $41 for a night in a suite in Scottsdale in June with the Entertainment card (50 percent off). It had a kitchenette, king-size bed, living room with queen sofa sleeper, tons of closets, and a bathroom. It also came with a free continental breakfast and newspaper, exercise room, Internet access, and pool, and was near golf courses. I was able to do the same when I went to Illinois. I stayed at a four-star hotel for $45 per night.

Airline Travel

You can find ample opportunities to save money on airline travel. Savings can involve using discount travel agencies, frequent-flyer coupons, vouchers sold at grocery stores, and even the Internet.

Many frugal travelers have snubbed travel agencies because they don't want to pay the agency's commissions. There are, however, many great deals that discount travel agencies can offer. The difference between a discount travel agency and a regular travel agency is that the discount agency has little to no overhead (no office, no receptionist, no glitzy ads). Sometimes the discount agencies add to the savings by buying blocks of seats at a low price and passing on the savings to us. Watch the newspaper for ads in the travel section for discount agencies.

Here are a few of those that buy blocks of seats and offer good discounts:

UniTravel Corp.	(800) 325-2222	*www.unitravel.com*
TFI Tours Intl.	(800) 745-8000	*www.lowestairprice.com*
1-800-FLY-CHEAP	(800) 359-2432	*www.flycheap.com*
Airhitch	(800) 282-1202	*www.air-hitch.org*

Travel agencies such as AAA offer good deals as well, including low fares on airlines, cruises, hotels, and trains. They also offer reasonable rates on package deals for destinations such as Alaska, Disneyland, and Disney World. If you are a AAA member, check out their travel services: 800-922-8228 or on their Web site at *www.aaa.com.*

Ever consider buying an airline ticket with your broccoli? That's becoming more popular these days. Airlines are teaming up with grocery stores and offering travel vouchers with a certain grocery total. This can be a great source of savings on airline tickets. With these vouchers, we were able to fly for less than it would have cost us to drive.

One of the most helpful areas for saving on airline travel comes from the Internet. It can provide the lowest prices with the least amount of time invested to find them. There are quite a few free travel Web sites as well as newsletters that you can subscribe to and receive through your e-mail. You can even make your reservations for most airlines, hotels, and car rentals via the Internet. Of course, as with any use of the Internet, do use caution. I never give my credit card number over the Internet but rather call the company's 800 number after I have obtained the price I saw on the Net, the flight number, date, and time.

One of my favorite travel Web sites is *www.cheaptickets.com.* This asks you what cities you want to travel between, what dates, and what time of day, and then lists the ten cheapest fares on all airlines. You can adjust the dates and times to see if it affects the price. Another one of my favorites is Arthur Frommer's Web site, *www.frommers.com,* which is an encyclopedia of information about any kind of travel you can imagine.

Another excellent use of the Internet for airline travel is the excess seats offered at super cheap fares for domestic and international travel. Basically, the airlines are trying to sell seats that would otherwise go unsold—so any money is better than no money for them, and you benefit too! These savings can range from 30 to 75 percent off regular fares.

The catch on these savings is that most require departure on the next Friday or Saturday and return on Sunday, Monday, or Tuesday. Some are more flexible with scheduling. There is also a limit as to which cities these offers are extended. They sometimes offer international fares for less than most regular domestic fares. If you can be flexible, spontaneous, and prepared to act on short notice, you can save a bundle on airfares.

Below are four major airline carriers that offer this service. Some are very easy to subscribe to—some are a little more complex. Once you subscribe, you will receive an e-mail with the airfare specials every Monday through Wednesday. Some carriers send you every special they offer. For other carriers, you can be more specific when you register and select departure and destination cities. Then these airlines will only send you notice of specials for the cities you selected. You can also call their 800 numbers on Wednesdays to hear what cheap seats are available.

- American Net SAAver
  (800) 344-6702
  www.americanair.com
- Continental CO.O.L.
  (800) 642-1617
  www.flycontinental.com/cool/
- Northwest CyberSaver Fares
  (800) 692-6961
  www.nwa.com/travel/cyber/cyber.html
- USAirways E-Savers
  (888) FLY-ESAVERS
  www.usair.com/travel/fares/esavers.htm

Other Tips for Air Travel

- Advertised specials may not be the cheapest. Ask if an airline will match a fare you saw; it may be necessary to speak to a supervisor.
- Check into the discount airlines such as Southwest or Sun

Country; they often offer the lowest fare to the cities they fly to.

- Ask if there is a discount for children. Most domestic airlines don't offer this, but a few offer a 50 percent discount for children under age two. Most airlines offer a discount on international flights for all children.

ONLY FOR THE TRULY ADVENTUROUS

There are some even more unusual ways to save money on travel, but these change the conventional ideas of what vacations mean. Most of us imagine a vacation to be on a plane or in a car or motel. There are some who travel by boat, but usually a cruise ship. To be different and save half off cruise ship rates, you could travel by sea freighter. These offer you a cabin room built for an officer (equivalent to a stateroom on a cruise ship) and three meals per day—but without the entertainment and endless food buffets. To try these options, call:

Freighter World Cruises   (800)531-7774   *freighterworld.com*
Maris   (800) 99-MARIS   *freighter-cruises.com*

If the usual vacation activities bore you, consider a vacation where you are a volunteer. There are several organizations that cater to travelers who would like to put their time to good use. *Volunteer Vacations* by Bill McMillan (Chicago Review Press, 1995) describes this type of vacation in detail and lists all of the organizations all over the world that you can help. Other places to look for opportunities to volunteer are mission agencies or your local church.

Some organizations offer travel packages to volunteer all over the world. Visit some of these sites for more information:

- *www.americanhiking.org*
- *www.crossculturalsolutions.org*
- *www.globalvolunteers.org*
- *www.sim.org*
- *www.habitat.org*
- *www.vfp.org*

*H*ELPFUL TRAVEL NUMBERS AND WEB SITES

American Automobile Association (AAA)	(800) 922-8228	*www.aaa.com*
Amtrak	(800) 387-1144	*www.amtrak.com*
Caravan Trips for RVs	(866) 324-8084	*www.rvcaravantours.com*
KOA cabins	(406) 248-7444	*www.koa.com*
National Park Service	(202) 208-4747	*www.nps.gov*
Steamboat Paddlewheel Vacations	(800) 543-1949	*www.deltaqueen.com*
Travel Coupons (Entertainment Books)	(313) 637-8400	*www.entertainment.com*
U.S. Chamber of Commerce	(202) 659-6000	*www.uschamber.org*
Western Union	(800) 325-6000	*www.westernunion.com*

RESOURCES

Hubbell, Beth. *Luxury Travel for the Unrich and Unfamous.* Jeremiah Publications, 1992.

Kaye, Evelyn. *Family Travel: Terrific New Vacations for Today's Families.* Blue Panda Publications, 1993.

Kaye, Evelyn. *Free Vacations and Bargain Adventures in the USA.* Blue Panda Publications, 1995

Ogintz, Eileen. *Are We There Yet?—A Parent's Guide to Fun Family Vacations.* Harper San Francisco, 1996.

Sutherland, Laura, and Valerie W. Deutsch. *The Best Bargain Family Vacations in the U.S.A.* St. Martin's, 1997.

Tristram, Claire, and Lucille Tristram. *Have Kid Will Travel: 101 Survival Strategies for Vacationing With Babies and Young Children.* Andrews McMeel Publishing, 1997.

CHAPTER SEVEN

Teaching Kids Financial Responsibility

Many persons have a wrong idea of what constitutes true happiness. It is not attained through self-gratification but through fidelity to a worthy purpose.

—Helen Keller

$ $ $

*I*t's no wonder kids think money flows endlessly: they see us go to the ATM machine and withdraw any amount we want—so they think. They don't see the budgeting and planning. Some people wonder how much kids should know about their parents' money management. Many parents have found that there are several creative ways to teach kids that the buck does stop—somewhere.

One idea is to involve the kids in some aspect of the bill paying. I am not comfortable with my children getting a great deal of exposure to our budget, so I pick small areas of our finances that they can learn about. For example, I tell them what the grocery allotment is and let them total up the food bill. This can be taken a step further by letting them plan the meals and snacks for a week to fit within that budget. Managing the family entertainment budget for one month is another way some parents teach financial management.

*A*LLOWANCES OR EARNED MONEY?

Another way to teach financial responsibility is to make sure kids have their own money to work and plan with. But should kids get an allowance or work for their money? Many parents feel that kids need early exposure to managing their money and should get an allowance, while others feel that all money should be earned. Some do a combination of both. Often those who feel that money should only come through work fear that an allowance not tied to chores is too much like welfare—they get something for nothing. These parents fear that their children will feel that money is an entitlement. They feel that earning money prepares them better for reality than an allowance would.

Common Jobs for Earning an Allowance

Clearing the table after a meal
Doing their own laundry
Making their own bed
Setting the table
Sweeping the floor
Taking out the trash

And then there are families who blend the two camps. Their kids get a small allowance and are required to do jobs for the rest of the money. This is what our family does. Our children receive a small allowance that is not tied to any jobs. They are required to do household chores just because they share our living space. For extra money, we keep a list on the refrigerator of jobs that provide a wage. Any time our children complain of not having enough money for an item, we remind them of their options. The wage is fair for each job. We don't pay them for the job unless the job is completed correctly. We do not withhold allowance for not doing chores, but rather withhold other privileges, such as television or computer time. We believe that the allowance and earned income teaches them how to handle money, and chores teach them responsibility.

What about borrowing? Some families believe that children should only spend their saved money, and they don't let them borrow money against future earnings or allowances. They believe that waiting to afford something is an important lesson; otherwise, they fear the kids will love those credit cards when they arrive. I like the intent of these families, but prefer a more moderate approach. I let my children borrow a small amount of their allowance if it's close to payment day. I don't usually loan more than one allowance amount or upcoming job's wage. The only exception I might make is if my kids see some great deal that may not be there tomorrow, and the upcoming income won't cover it. Under these circumstances I might buy the item, but not give it to them until they have earned or saved the amount due. I offer more of a layaway plan than a loan.

We started our kids with an allowance as early as age three to help them learn. The amount was small but enough to teach the basics of tithing, saving, and spending wisely. To help those who want to give an allowance but aren't sure how much to give, I have included a sidebar on the next page with some suggestions. Each family should determine their own allowance levels, taking family earnings and the child's expenses into account.

Common Jobs for Earning Extra Money

Baby-sitting
Cleaning bathrooms
Dusting
Gardening
Mowing lawns
Organizing the basement
Painting walls or fences
Raking leaves
Shoveling snow
Sorting/recycling
Sweeping the walk
Washing the car
Washing or folding family laundry
Washing windows
Word processing

I have found that kids who have no source of their own income tend to beg and nag for things they want. These kids need to have a source of money, such as an allowance or job, so that they can budget and spend within their own means.

Whether you choose to give an allowance or not, the best help you can give your kids is to make a plan (or budget) for their needs and wants. I'm shocked at how few (2 percent) parents require their kids to have a budget. Help them write down what they have and what they hope to or need to buy. Help them learn to make their money last until needed, setting aside a certain amount each week to meet their goals (a bike, a toy, a game ticket, gifts for others, etc.). Some parents even encourage their kids to divide their money among four categories: tithing/charity (10 percent), savings for smaller items (30 percent), big-ticket-item savings (30 percent), and mad money for anything they want (30 percent).

How Much Allowance Should I Give?

Families vary on the amount of allowance to give. Many give $1 per week for every year of age (a ten-year-old would receive $10 per week). Others give what they can afford, with that being as little as 50¢ per month. Give an amount that you can afford and that is fair for the child.

Take the time to use teachable moments in stores or on outings. I have my son help at the store by asking him to find the cheapest item of what I need or have him keep a running total of our expenditures so we don't exceed our budget.

Other things you can do to help kids learn how to manage money:

- Open a savings account for those big-ticket items.
- Adopt a needy family and have everyone (parents included) donate something each week that would meet their needs.
- Let the kids see you put something back because you can't afford it.
- Fix your own attitude about money: get your spending under control, stop fighting over money with your spouse, don't use credit.
- Don't pay kids for scoring on their athletic teams—you send the wrong message.
- Consider turning off the television: the commercials breed materialism in kids. They believe they "need" the toys they see.
- If the kids insist on a name-brand clothing item, let them make up the difference between the off-brand version and the more expensive item with their earned money.
- Remember that their money is their money. Let them make the decisions on what to use it for, and let them live with their decisions. This is how they learn best.
- Don't give them more than you agreed upon.
- Don't withhold allowance or earned money as a disciplinary tool.

Teenagers need to start taking responsibility for their living expenses since they will soon be managing their own lives. Start giving them money for clothing, doctor bills, and whatever else you agree they should control. Help them set up a budget for those items, and periodically check on their budget. Many financial counselors recommend parents still manage the cost of meals at home, shelter, and utilities.

The parents I talked to agreed: it is most important to stick to whatever plan we chose. If you give in to the "gimmes," they won't stop when you say no. They will keep pestering until we give in because they've seen us do it before.

Help for Younger Kids

The Berenstain Bears Get the Gimmes by Stan and Jan Berenstain

Trouble With Money by Stan and Jan Berenstain

Freckle Juice by Judy Blume

Help for Older Kids

Consumer Reports created a Web site just for kids. Its aim is to help kids think about money and spending. It has a section of questions and answers about money, a toy test section (just like the grown-up magazine), and a section to help kids analyze advertisements. This Web site appeals to ages 8–14.

Zillions: Consumer Reports for Kids—www.zillions.org

RESOURCES

Blue, Ron, and Judy Blue. *Raising Money-Smart Kids: How to Teach Your Children the Secrets of Earning, Saving, Investing, and Spending Wisely.* Thomas Nelson, 1992.

Bodnar, Janet. *Kiplinger's Money-Smart Kids.* Dove Books, 1995.

Briles, Judith. *Raising Money-Wise Kids.* Moody Press, 1996.

Burgeson, Nancy. *Money Book for Kids.* Troll Associates, 1991.

Burkett, Larry, and Rick Osborne. *Financial Parenting: Showing Kids That Money Matters.* Moody Press, 1999.

Godfrey, Neales S., and Carolina Edwards. *Money Doesn't Grow on Trees: A Parent's Guide to Raising Financially Responsible Children.* Fireside Publishing, 1994.

Kay, Ellie. *Money Doesn't Grow on Trees: Teaching Your Kids the Value of a Buck.* Bethany House, 2002.

Otfinoski, Steve. *The Kid's Guide to Money: Earning It, Saving It, Spending It, Growing It, Sharing It.* Scholastic Trade, 1996.

Ryan, Bernard, and Elizabeth Lewin. *Simple Ways to Help Your Kids Become Dollar-Smart: 125 Ways to Teach Children the Value of Money.* Walker & Company, 1994.

CHAPTER EIGHT

Pets

The dog who meets with a good master is the happier of the two.

—Maurice Maeterlinck

$ $ $

*K*ids and pets seem to go together naturally. A loving pet matched with the energy of a child can be a wonderful combination. Sometimes, however, the match isn't made in heaven. That's why it's important to make sure that the type of pet and the child are matched carefully. Most families select a pet for companionship or because the animal is fun to watch. Knowing your family's needs and preferences will help select the right type of pet. Later in the chapter you'll find tips on being frugal without compromising your pet's care.

CHOOSING THE RIGHT PET

If observing a pet's cute or calming behavior is a main priority, then fish, small caged mammals, or reptiles are the best choice. If companionship is more important, then dogs or cats would be good selections. Some children are rough with animals, and parents need to make sure the pet can put up with that type of behavior. Some animals will take it well, while others will resort to bizarre behavior such as biting themselves or perhaps biting the child. For example, a high-strung lap dog would not be a good match for a rambunctious toddler.

Many families select dogs for their family pet. These are usually a great addition to the family. But before rushing out and getting one, make sure that all of the dog's needs are considered. Are the children home enough to play with it, walk it, and love it? Or are they busy with after-school activities? Does your family travel often? Finding care for animals while you're away is one of the top complaints of pet ownership. Does the family have room for the pet? A dog needs a place to run for exercise.

Another thing to consider is whether the family can afford the animal. Expenses include the weekly food bill, vet checkups, shots, training, etc. A dog costs an average of $13,000 during its lifetime—$4,500 for food and $3,400 in vet bills. The rest is used for toys, leashes, training, and housing. The average pet owner visits the pet store four to eight times per year. Most of these trips are for food, but 45 percent of all pet owners say they buy toys and gifts as well. We'll come back to vet bills later in the chapter.

Another consideration is whether or not the temperament of the desired breed matches that of the children and family. Certain types of dogs require lots of human contact and stimulation. This is especially true of Labradors and golden retrievers, the two most common breeds chosen for family dogs. Several books on breeds are available at the library or a bookstore. One highly recommended by dog trainers is *Your Purebred Puppy* by Michelle Lowell. Even though you probably won't be shopping for a purebred, understanding how each breed tends to behave will help you make an informed choice.

Pets Owned by People

Dogs	37 percent
Cats	32 percent
Birds	6 percent
Small mammals	5 percent
Fish	3 percent
Horses	3 percent

Many families start with the smaller mammals first, namely rats, guinea pigs, hamsters, gerbils, and rabbits. These make good starter pets since they cost very little and the family can see how the children will handle the responsibility of pet ownership. We have several pets, including a dog, cats, and rats. Many people are surprised at our choice of rats for a pet. They are surprisingly social and affectionate, even-tempered, and inexpensive to purchase, house, and feed. If cared for well, they live up to five years. An animal shelter veterinarian suggested rats to us as great pets for younger children. She had raised five boys and said rats were the best of all the pets they had tried. We tried it and were pleased.

ℱood

Feeding a pet often deters people from owning one. If you have a ninety-pound dog, it will eat as much as or more than a child does. To help cut back on the expense of purchased pet food, many pet owners resort to table scraps. This is not recommended since an animal's nutritional needs differ greatly from humans. Some people buy the cheapest brand of pet food they can find using coupons and sales. This may be necessary if the budget is strained. However, many nutritionists caution against buying cheap brands of pet food. They believe the canned food is made of diseased or old meat, with added coloring and flavoring to make it look fresh.

Their opinion of dry food isn't much better: it often includes non-nutritious filler such as ash. Some studies have shown that the protein in canned pet food is minimally usable to pets, with pets absorbing only 25 percent of the protein listed on the can. These researchers explain that the crude protein can be made from ligaments, hair, feather meal, and waste. As a result, the pets are malnourished and may develop skin disorders and diseases.

We discovered firsthand what these nutritionists meant while we were caring for a friend's cat. We had the cat for several months and wondered why he acted so strangely. One moment he would purr and rub your leg and the next he would bite, growl, and attack. My son remembered what we had learned about canned pet food having additives and wondered if the additives affected the cat. So we bought some dry food from a reputable manufacturer and stopped feeding the cat the canned food. The cat's personality changed within a day or two.

These same nutritionists recommend adding raw meats and vegetables occasionally to the canine and feline diet. Pets fed the raw foods supposedly are healthier and livelier. This in turn lowers the vet bills. These experts believe that the animals' immune systems cannot function if there are not some raw ingredients in their diet a few times per week. If you choose this approach, please research this method further. Some books on the topic are listed in the resources section of this book.

Whether we agree with these nutritionists or not, there are some ways to avoid the high prices of health-food-store brands of pet food. One way is to make the food yourself. I am not advocating the use of table scraps for dogs or cats. This would be unhealthy for them and lead to disease and obesity in the pet. I am talking about making nutritionally balanced meals for your dog or cat.

When we lived overseas, we couldn't buy canned or dry pet food (pets weren't kept in these countries) so we made our dog's food. We boiled meat bones and fresh meat strips with rice, oil, and some herbs or spices. I later found that this is a more common practice than I thought. Just as with human food, homemade is usually healthier.

Doggie Diner or Kitty Kafe

Many of the recipes listed for cats can also be used for dogs, and vice versa.

Vegetarian Delight

2 oz. tofu
½ cup cooked rice
½ cup cooked corn
1 egg yolk
Mash the tofu or dice into little bites. Mix the rest of the ingredients with the tofu.

Basic Meal

1 lb. dry brown rice
1 large meat bone
½ cup parsley
water to cover
¼ cup olive, canola, or safflower oil
Combine all ingredients except the oil. Bring to a boil, then

lower the temperature and simmer for 1 hour, or until the rice is tender. Drain excess water and add the oil. This can be refrigerated and used throughout the week.

Doggie Deluxe Hamburger

10 oz. lean ground beef
1 slice whole-wheat bread, crumbled
1 egg
1 T. chopped parsley
Combine the ingredients and form into a patty. Broil or pan-fry until done.

Good Morning Pooch

4 cups rice crisp cereal
2 scrambled eggs
1 cup parsnips
1 T. olive oil
Combine in a bowl. Store any unused portion in the refrigerator.

Dry Pet Food

1½ cups whole-wheat flour
1½ cups rye flour
1½ cups brown rice flour (grind dry rice in blender)
1 cup wheat germ
1 tsp. garlic powder
1 tsp. kelp powder
4 T. vegetable oil
1¼ cups beef or chicken broth
After combining the dry ingredients, slowly add the oil and broth, stirring as you add. Roll the dough into a thin sheet on a cookie sheet and bake at 350 degrees 15 minutes (or until light brown). After it is cool, break into small pieces. For small dogs or cats, break into smaller pieces. Store in the refrigerator.

Options: For other flavors, add a can (15 oz.) of salmon or mackerel, or add a pound of ground chicken meat or livers to the dough before baking.

Dog Biscuits

⅔ cup fat (saved chicken fat, bacon drippings, or
    shortening such as Crisco)
1¼ cups hot water (or soup stock)
2 eggs
4 tsp. honey or brown sugar
1 tsp. salt
6 cups flour
1 cup powdered milk

    Combine water and fat in a large mixing bowl. Mix in the eggs, honey, and salt. Add the flour and dry milk and stir to make dough. Mix for a few minutes until well blended. Roll onto a floured surface (like you were making biscuits) to ½-inch thick. Cut into small (2-inch) shapes. Bake at 325 degrees for 50 minutes, or until brown. Let biscuits cool and leave uncovered for several hours to harden. Store in an airtight container in the refrigerator. (This recipe was contributed by Laura Williams' *Frugal Living Newsletter,* which is no longer in print. Her latest endeavor is making soaps: *www.showertreatsoap.com.*)

Kitty Salad

1 hard-boiled egg, chopped
3 T. boiled fish, chopped
1 tsp. milk or sour cream
    Mix these together.

Treat Time

3 saltine crackers, or 2 T. cooked oats, cooked rice, or millet
3 T. smoked fish, diced
1 T. steamed vegetables
1 tsp. sour cream, cottage cheese, milk, or oil
    Crumble the crackers. Mix the rest of the ingredients with the crackers.

Bowser's Biscuits

    A favorite treat of our dog is doggie biscuits. We use a regular biscuit recipe (for humans) and add one flavor to it (1 cup cheese, 4 cloves garlic, ½ cup barbecue sauce, or ½ cup honey).

We then roll the biscuit thin (½-inch) and cut it into shapes. Bake it the same time as a regular biscuit recipe calls for so the doggie biscuits are crunchy. Inexpensive, healthy, and yummy!

Kitten Meal

⅓ cup cooked oatmeal
2 tsp. carrot, steamed and minced
1 T. meat, minced
¼ tsp. milk, warmed
2 tsp. wheat germ or 1 tsp. oil

Blend all ingredients well in a bowl.

If your cat is finicky, try mixing a teaspoon of chicken fat into the food or drizzle some of the liquid from a can of tuna over the food to encourage him to eat. If your cat is overweight, tripe or tofu is an excellent alternative for meat. They are fat-free but high in protein.

Because kittens need twice the amount of protein as adult cats, leave a bowl of food out at all times so they can eat throughout the day.

What Is the Biological Value of Your Pet Food?

The biological value of a food is a measure of how much of the protein is actually used by the body. This is not to be confused with the "crude protein" that is on most labels. An item can be a protein (such as hair, hooves, etc.) but it may not be digestible protein. Here are some numbers that show how much of a protein is useable to the pet:

Eggs	100%
Fish	92%
Beef	78%
Milk	78%
Wheat	60%

When you read the ingredient label on pet food, the first ingredient is the main component of the food. Since it is the main ingredient, it should be a digestible source of protein (biological value) and not a grain, like corn or wheat. It would require extra food each day of a grain-based food in order for the pet to meet its protein requirements.

Feeding Small Mammals

For a small mammal, such as a hamster or rabbit, try to use the natural things in your home before resorting to the expensive bags of food sold in stores. We use the peelings from carrots and potatoes, the greens from the carrot tops, a leaf or two of lettuce, apple peelings, whole-wheat bread crusts, raw oats, etc., for our rats. Most of these are usually destined for the compost pile, but they are very nutritious. And our pets love it! Our food bill for the rats is around $25 per year.

VETERINARIANS AND HEALTH CARE

Veterinarian bills can be the largest expense of owning pets. But there are ways to shave some of the cost without compromising care. If you choose one of the four-legged creatures that requires vaccinations, try to find cheaper sources than your local vet. Many pet stores host mobile vaccine clinics that run about $10 to $15 per shot. One company that offers these mobile vaccination clinics is Pet Vaccine Services. To see if it services your area, call (800) 3-DOG-CAT. Other sources of inexpensive vaccines are the local county department of animal regulation and control, the humane society, and low-cost spay and neuter clinics.

Vaccines are just one way to reduce vet bills. Here are some other ways to save:

- Keep the animal healthy through proper diet and nutrition.
- Check around for vet prices—they vary greatly (make sure the vet is reputable as well).
- Get books and videos from the library that demonstrate:
  dental cleaning at home
  grooming
  nail clipping
  treating simple infections

Helpful Pet Hot Lines

For general information on treating your pet, try these hot lines:

- Pet Lover's Helpline (900) 776-0007
  Recorded messages on more than three hundred topics concerning your pet. Costs 97¢ per minute. Obtain a free copy of the directory by calling the phone number.
- National Animal Poison Control Center (800) 548-2423 (emergency number)
  Charges $30 per case and accepts credit cards

or call (900) 680-0000, which charges $20 for the first five minutes of advice, then $2.95 per minute.

- National Dog Registry Helps locate lost pets (800) 637-6347
- Pet Loss Support Helpline (530) 752-4200 or (900) 565-1526
  Offers counseling and support on the loss of a pet
- Animal Behavior Helpline (415) 554-3075
  Offers advice on dog and cat behavior problems

Online services are available by most Internet providers. Do a search on your carrier by using key words such as *pet forum, animal forum, dogs, cats, pet behavior, pet training, ask-the-vet, reptiles, exotic pets, pet stories,* and *pet support groups.*

Average Vet Bills per Year	
32% of families spend	$150–350
29% of families spend	$ 50–150
16% of families spend	$350–500

Fleas

When we lived in California, the number one pest was fleas. Our vet said his main source of income came from all the flea dips and products he sold to rid our homes and pets of the little creatures. Fleas can feel like a curse, especially if you are unable to use the chemical solutions available for this problem.

Here are some homemade remedies that worked for us when our pet and home had fleas:

For fleas and eggs in the carpets:

- Sprinkle Borax all over the carpet, especially around the edges. Work it into the carpet. Let it sit for three days, then vacuum.
- Sprinkle boric acid where the wall and carpet meet. Fleas like tight places and lay eggs there. You can buy this in bulk at a hardware store (or drug store sometimes), or you can pay more and buy it at a pet store under the name of The Terminator.
- Sprinkle diatomaceous earth (DE) around the carpet and crevices where the wall and floor meet. This cuts their skin and dehydrates them. Don't buy the pool supply type of DE,

which is dangerous if inhaled.

- Steam clean the carpet, then vacuum daily for a few days. The hot water kills most of the eggs and fleas. The others will hatch a few days later from the heat.
- After vacuuming, remove the bag and seal it in a plastic bag. Set in the sun to bake the trapped fleas.
- Lay fresh eucalyptus branches and leaves around the edges of the carpets in the house. It's a natural repellent, and they'll leave in a few days. Bay leaves are supposed to be effective as well.

For fleas on the pet:

- Use a flea comb, dipping it in a bowl of soapy water or rubbing alcohol after catching the fleas in the comb.
- Simmer sliced lemons for forty-five minutes, then cool and strain the solution. Wet the pet thoroughly.

RESOURCES

Bowman, Linda. *Free Stuff and Good Deals for Your Pet.* Santa Monica Press, 2001.

Guidry, Virginia P. *Pet Care on a Budget.* Howell Book House, 1997.

Palike, Liz. *The Consumer's Guide to Cat Food: What's in Cat Food, Why It's There, and How to Choose the Best Food for Your Cat.* Hungry Minds, 1997.

Papai, Franki. *The Cat Lover's Cookbook.* St. Martin's Press, 1993.

Pitcairn, Richard. *Dr. Pitcairn's Complete Guide to Natural Health for Dogs and Cats.* Rodale Press, 1995.

CHAPTER NINE

Money, Money

Now is no time to think of what you do not have;
think of what you can do with what there is.

—Ernest Hemingway

$ $ $

*B*ankruptcies are near record highs. Consumer credit counseling is a booming business. Debt has become an acceptable form of supporting a desired lifestyle. Some people have taken control of their finances by digging out of debt, budgeting, and actually saving some money. These people had to make a conscious decision in order to make this work. For some it took a wake-up call.

Getting a call from a collection agency or being turned down for a loan can provide that needed shock. Sometimes it takes the anger of a loved one to help us stop and see the deep water we have shopped our way into. Some of us ignore the call and keep living beyond our means. Others see they are out of control and get help.

Help can come in many forms. Credit counseling, budgeting, debt consolidation, and refinancing a mortgage are some of the tools used. Some are more profitable and reliable than others. Let's explore each of these tools and see their helpfulness and pitfalls.

*D*EBT

Achieving a no-debt lifestyle is a rewarding feeling. The hard work it takes to get there makes the blessings worthwhile. Without debt, you are free: free to stay home, make plans for a future event, go back to school, change careers, or expand your family. Debt can sap the life out of us as we worry and fret over bills. It instigates more fights between spouses than any other topic. It leads to much loss of personal property. It is something to be avoided and to make a serious effort to be rid of.

Making more money doesn't usually solve the dilemma. Statistics have shown that the more we make, the higher our debt goes. Let's look at the facts:

- Forty percent of households earning $10,000 or less carry consumer debt;
- Sixty percent of households earning up to $25,000 carry consumer debt;
- Ninety percent of households earning $50,000 or more carry consumer debt.
- Over the past few years consumer debt has risen 10 percent more than at any other time in U.S. history.
- The average consumers devote 20 percent of their take-home pay to debt (this does not include mortgages).[1]

Financial analysts speculate that the debt has risen because we are hopeful for the future economy and are spending today, planning on paying it off in the future. Over half of consumer credit counseling clients admit that their debt was caused by poor money management (only one-fifth claimed unemployment as the cause). This attitude can lead to our financial undoing. We can't bank on what tomorrow will bring. These same analysts have calculated that it would take an average annual income of $200,000 for a household to pay off the debt it is currently accumulating.[2]

This same "spend now/pay later" attitude reveals something else about us. It suggests that we do not accept the limits of our income; we are living beyond our means. It suggests that we feel that we deserve more than we can afford.

In our first month of marriage, Beau and I decided that we had a debt problem (a common newlywed realization). The carefree spending of our single years now was a large mess. We agreed that we had to plan a budget that included paying down those debts. To start the new financial lifestyle, we had a credit card cutting ceremony. We have a picture of this ceremony in our scrapbook, with Beau sitting in the middle of a pile of cut up credit cards. We kept one credit card but use it only for emergencies, and we use a few gas cards.

Not everyone needs to cut up his or her cards. Some have more willpower than others. If you lack the willpower but want to have a card for emergencies, leave the card at home. A true emergency can wait while you go home and get the card.

$\mathscr{B}$UDGETING

One of the first steps toward taking financial control is to make a budget. A budget is a plan of attack. And no war can be won without a plan. There are many budget planning books on the market, and deciding where to start can be confusing. The best ones I have found are listed in the resources at the end of the chapter.

Debt Statistics

- Eighty-nine percent of Americans use at least one credit card, with the average cardholder having three or four bankcards (VISA, MasterCard, Diners Club) and eight to ten other credit cards.
- The amount that Americans owe on loans for houses, cars, credit cards, and other purchases adds up to nearly 100 percent of their annual income after taxes. That's up from 75 percent in 1992, after the last recession ended.[3]
- A record 1,398,864 personal bankruptcies were filed during 2001 as reported by the Administrative Office of the U.S. Courts.
- Americans carried $701 billion in credit card balances at mid-year 2001, which comes to an average credit card balance of $8,488 per household, reports CardWeb.Com.
- The average U.S. family is spending more than $1,000 per year in interest and fees.

Assessing the Damage

Most financial counselors suggest some basic steps to begin a debt reduction plan. First, they recommend that we assess the damage. We need to look at all of our obligations and spending habits. Only then can we make a budget and plan our spending.

To get started with our obligations, it is recommended that we do the following:

1. List expenses for each month. Include:
   - Federal taxes
   - State taxes
   - Social security taxes
   - Mortgage/rent
   - Household expenses
   - Homeowner's insurance (calculate monthly cost if annual)
   - Property taxes or homeowner association fees
   - Medical/dental insurance (calculate monthly cost if annual)
   - Life insurance (calculate monthly cost if annual)
   - Auto insurance (calculate monthly cost if annual)
   - Auto payments
   - Child support
   - Daycare
   - School costs
   - Debts (list each individually: credit cards, loans)
   - Utilities
   - Food
   - Entertainment (include cable TV)
   - Magazine and newspaper subscriptions
   - Book or video clubs
   - Clothing store charge accounts
   - Doctor/dentist bills
   - Past-due taxes
   - Birthdays and holiday gifts
   - Savings
   - Hair care
   - Allowances

If you do not know what you spend for some of the variable categories, such as food, go over checkbook entries and receipts for the last month or two to get an accurate total. Being honest about what you spend is very important at this point.

2. List all income for the month. Include:
   - Salary
   - Rent income
   - Interest
   - Dividends

- Child support
- Other

3. Compare your income to your expenses. If you have more income than expenses, you are blessed. Use that blessing constructively. Save for a child's college fund, start a helping fund for less fortunate friends and their emergencies, or invest for your retirement.

   If your expenses exceed your income, here are a few things to look at before you start panicking:

- Are you keeping accurate records?
- Do you balance the checkbook often?
- Have you spent money on unplanned impulse items?
- Have you planned for birthday and holiday gifts?

Making a Budget

Now that you know what you spend and earn, putting yourself on a money diet is the next step. Deciding where to trim and what to leave alone can be confusing. What should your clothing allotment be? How much should you be spending on food? What is a reasonable entertainment amount?

Financial counselors will have their own answers to these questions. What is reasonable may also vary depending on what part of the country you live in. For example, in the San Francisco Bay Area it is common for people to spend 50 percent of their income on mortgage payments or rent, whereas 25 percent is more common in the Midwest. The following general guidelines give you a place to start.

Since every household has varying needs, adjust these percentages as needed. Some may need daycare, while others have

Ways to Avoid Impulse Shopping
- Use layaway purchasing. It requires you to have the money before you buy something. It also helps you think about whether you really need an item.
- Wait thirty days before you decide to buy anything.
- Establish a rule that you and your spouse cannot buy anything over $5 without discussing it first.

greater medical needs. Others may know that their car will probably die in a few years so they should be saving now for a new one. Adjust the numbers to fit your needs, taking from some areas and adding in others where needed.

Suggested Budget Percentages (after taxes and tithe)[4]

Housing (rent or mortgage, utilities, insurance, taxes, maintenance)	38 percent
Food	12 percent
Cars (payments, maintenance, insurance)	15 percent
Debts	5 percent
Insurance (life and medical)	5 percent
Entertainment (include cable TV)	5 percent
Clothing	5 percent
Medical/dental (bills)	5 percent
Savings	5 percent
Miscellaneous	5 percent

Here is a sample monthly budget for a household income of $35,000, using the recommended percentages from the above chart:

Gross Monthly Income	**$2,916**
Expenses	
taxes (28 percent—may vary)	816
tithe	290
Net Monthly Income	**$1,810**
Budgeted Expense Catagories	
household	660
(mortgage/rent, household expenses, property taxes, homeowner association fees, utilities, telephone, maintenance)	
insurance	90
(homeowner's, life)	
medical	90
(medical/dental insurance, doctor/ dentist bills)	

automobile	270
(insurance, payments, maintenance, gasoline)	
debts (list each individually)	90
(department stores, VISA or MasterCard, clothing store charge accounts, past-due taxes, child support)	
clothing	90
food	250
entertainment	90
(cable TV, magazine subscriptions, book or video clubs, vacations)	
savings	90
miscellaneous	90
(allowances, haircuts, dry cleaning, gifts, cash for spending)	

Sticking to a Budget

Making a budget is much easier than sticking to one. It is much like a food diet: we plan and intend to stick to the diet, but we keep on eating those brownies because they taste so good. Spending is fun. The daily temptation to buy things is strong. Advertisements constantly tell us that we aren't complete unless we have this or that or that we are "missing out" or "less cool" than everyone else if we don't modernize and consume. We get tired of saying no and we spend. A more dangerous tendency is to have the attitude that "we deserve this."

To stay motivated with your budget, try these tricks:

- Remember the reason you are budgeting in the first place. Think about the debt you had or the plans you are trying to make.
- Go to the bank once a week and withdraw what the budget allots for that week. Do not return to the bank or ATM until the next week. Only spend what you have.
- If you have any leftover money at the end of each week, put it in a bank or special envelope and save it for a special occasion or purchase.

- Don't go to the mall unless you have a specific reason. Only one in four people in the malls is there for a particular purchase, and 93 percent of American girls say store hopping is their favorite activity.[5]

Ways to Reduce Debt

Sometimes our debt considerably exceeds our income, and any attempt at tweaking the budget can't cover the deficit. Before considering a second income, look at some of the alternatives to getting your debt down. Here are some of the tools people use:

Free Budget Planners

Consumer Alert, a national consumer group founded in 1977, offers a free two-page budget planner. It contains a budget worksheet and some suggestions on starting a budget. To get this, send a self-addressed, stamped envelope to:
Consumer Alert
Budget Planner Offer
1001 Connecticut Ave NW
Suite 1128
Washington, DC 20036
Or download it from their Web site:
*www.consumeralert.org/pubs/
commonsense/Budget98.htm*

Debt Pay-Down Plan

In a debt pay-down plan, you give each creditor a payment each month. Plan on paying off the loan with the lowest balance first. When that bill is paid off, take the amount that was being applied to that monthly bill and add it to the amount being paid to the bill with the next lowest balance. Each time you pay one off, roll that amount over to the next one. This has a snowball effect, adding momentum to the next

bill, and so on, until they are all gone!

Here is a sample of a debt pay-down plan:

Bill	Balance Payment	Months							
		1	2	3	4	5	6	...	10
A	$75	25	25	25					
B	$600	50	50	50	75	75	75	...	
C	$1500	100	100	100	100	100	100	...	175

Notice that the monthly payments increase as the previous debt is paid off.

Other Tips:

Try to surpass the minimum due if you can. Paying a little extra adds up. For example, if you had a credit card balance of $3,000 at a finance rate of 15 percent and you paid the minimum each month, it would take you 30 years to pay it off. The total amount paid would end up being over $10,000. If, however, you added $5 to the minimum payment, you would pay off the balance in half the time and with half the total amount paid.

Is there a credit card with a lower annual percentage rate (APR) than the one you are paying? If so, transfer your balance to that card, but do not spend more. Close the other account. This just reduces the amount of finance charge you will be paying as you pay down the debt. Don't be fooled by the low introductory rates that inflate in a few months. Choose a card with an interest rate that remains low until you can pay it off. Don't keep on transferring the balance from account to account instead of paying the debt.

If you have a savings account, many financial counselors recommend using it to pay down the debt. The reason is that savings accounts earn much less interest than the interest being charged by your credit cards. You may consider selling some assets to pay off the debt (jewelry, extra real estate, stocks, a second car, antiques, newer car for an older one). Ask a lender if they will offer you a discount on the interest rate if you make payments automatically from your checking account. And avoid late payments on any account. The finance charges will wipe out any progress that you made on paying down the balance.

Finding Hidden Money

When I quit my job, we lost 50 percent of our income. We didn't move or sell a car. When we looked at our budget and the deficit we had, we found extra money for some bills by redoing our food budget. We cut our groceries by 60 percent and used that extra money for other expenses. The specific steps of how we did it are in *Miserly Moms—Living on One Income in a Two-Income Economy*.

Refinance Your Mortgage

By refinancing your mortgage, you take out a loan that will cover your mortgage as well as all of your debts. This reduces your overall payments, but extends the amount of your debt over thirty years. You also lose all equity you have built up and start all over each time you refinance. I know people who do this regularly so that they can continue to live beyond their means. When they retire, they will have a rude surprise with large monthly payments to make throughout their golden years.

If you decide to go this route, keep a few things in mind:

- Don't use this option often. Your debt is still there, just masked in another payment.
- Don't use the lower payments as an excuse to spend more.
- It isn't cost effective unless you can get a rate at least 1 percent lower than your current mortgage and you plan on staying in the house for at least two years (this covers closing costs).

Debtors Support Group

There is a support group for debtors, fashioned after the twelve-step program of Alcoholics Anonymous. It's called Debtors Anonymous. They have weekly meetings to cope with debt problems. For a group in your area, contact:

Debtors Anonymous
P.O. Box 920888
Needham, MA 02492-0009
(781) 453-2743
www.debtorsanonymous.org

Credit Counseling

Credit counselors act as a liaison between you and your creditors. They may get the creditors to agree to a lower monthly payment or not to make collection proceedings. Credit counselors will take your bills along with your income and be in control of both each month. You will be given an allowance to use for your other expenses. The creditors tend to respond to credit counselors because they believe the debtor is serious about repaying if she has hired one, and creditors have come to know and trust credit counselors.

Credit counseling services are not a quick fix for your spending woes. The total amount of your debt is still there. Just because your monthly payments are lower does not mean the debt is a smaller amount.

Some pitfalls to credit counseling should be considered before going this route:

- Credit counseling is unregulated in many states. This can leave people at the mercy of con artists who are really selling high-interest credit cards.
- Check to see if the credit counselor is certified by the National Certification Board of the National Foundation for Consumer Credit (800) 388-2227.
- The credit counseling fee should be no more than $10–$25 per month, since the counselors are usually funded by banks or other organizations.

Helpful Numbers

Consumer Credit Counseling Service (CCCS) (800) 388-CCCS: A national non-profit organization that offers free and low-cost credit counseling and education

National Center for Financial Education (619) 232-8811: Offers free booklets on debt reduction *www.ncfe.org*

National Foundation for Credit Counseling (800) 388-2227 *www.nfcc.org*

Christian Credit Counseling *www.christianccc.org*

Debt Consolidation

Debt consolidation is taking a new loan out to cover all of your debts. Your monthly payment will be lower than the combined bills. Not everyone considers this option to be very helpful for the following reasons:

- Fees for these loans average 10 percent of the loan amount (more debt!).
- The interest rates on these loans may be higher than your credit card is currently charging.
- You are replacing an unsecured credit card debt with a loan against your home. A credit card company has little recourse in collecting their debt, whereas defaulting on a loan with a

home as collateral can lead to the loss of your home.

- The loan may hinder your ability to sell your home or refinance a mortgage since the loan's value may exceed your equity.
- The interest on these loans may not be deductible.

Identity Theft

If you have had your identity stolen and debt incurred in your name, write a notarized letter to the creditor stating that it is not your doing.

To prevent it from happening, take these precautions:

- Tear up those preapproved credit card offers.
- NEVER give any personal information to a telephone solicitor.
- Don't write (or let someone else write) credit card numbers on a check.
- Don't give out your social security number unless you agree with the need to have it.
- Check your credit report annually. Equifax (800) 685-1111, Experian (888) 397-3742, Trans Union (800) 888-4213. Many credit reporting agencies will give each person a free report each year. Check for:
  accounts that are not yours
  accounts that you closed but
    show activity
  past-due accounts
  unpaid balances that you
    thought were paid

- With a debt pay-down plan or CCCS intervention you may have paid off your debts in a few years. But with the loan, you have spread the same debts out over twenty years.
- Be careful that the agent selling you the loan isn't an attorney who tries to convince people of their need for his services in bankruptcy court.

Bankruptcy

This is not an option that I would encourage, since I believe that we need to be responsible for ourselves and our actions. However, many people feel they are cornered and, according to the National Bankruptcy Review Commission, more than a million households file for bankruptcy each year. And the number rises each year. Most causes for bankruptcy are listed as credit card debt.

Bankruptcy is often referred to as filing Chapter 7, 11, or 13. Let's look at each type.

Chapter 7 is liquidation of all assets and distribution of the money to the creditors. All debts are discharged, whether or not there was enough money to cover the debts. Occasionally a portion of the home equity is spared, but a lawyer can explain your situation best. This action gives the debtor a fresh start. This works for most debts but does not cover debts for:

child support or alimony

taxes owed for the past three years (older than three years are covered)

student loans

money owed for intentional and willful misconduct

secured debts (such as home loans)

Chapter 11 is a reorganization of finances that is usually used by businesses but can be used by individuals. Chapter 11 allows the debtors to remain in control of all possessions and businesses and continue to manage the estate themselves, all while working with the creditors. This is very expensive, with filing fees and lawyers, and can take several months to settle. The goal of Chapter 11 is to settle on a repayment plan with your creditors. This can usually be achieved with less money and take less time by filing Chapter 13.

You Don't Have to Take It

If you are being harassed by a bill collection agency, you can stop those phone calls and letters. Under the Fair Debt Collection Practices Act, collectors must stop calling and writing you if you write them a letter requesting this. Half of the states in the U.S. also require this same practice of the original loan issuer. If they do not comply, contact the Federal Trade Commission, Washington, DC 20580.

Chapter 13 is another form of reorganization. It repays all debts in full but allows you more time to do it. By filing Chapter 13, you can get up to sixty months to repay existing debts. You are given a trustee to whom you give a monthly payment for all debts, and the trustee distributes the payments. In order to file for Chapter 13, you must have a steady income and your unsecured debts (credit cards) must not exceed $250,000.

Since any of these is a serious step to take and laws vary by state, consulting an attorney before making this decision is essential. Keep in mind that a debtor who files bankruptcy has damaged his credit rating for up to ten years. This is in addition to the emotional turmoil it creates. For more information on bankruptcy, contact the Bureau of Consumer Protection—Office of Consumer and Business Education at (202) 326-3650.

SAVING

Many Americans do not have a savings account. For those who do save, the amount saved is a much smaller percentage of their income than in most other progressive nations. This lack of savings usually leaves us lacking when an emergency hits. And we turn to borrowing money in order to survive.

Starting the saving habit is easy. We need to start putting money aside each month, no matter how small the amount. If we start small, it is easier to ease into the saving habit. And if that money is used wisely, it could grow and provide you with even more of a cushion.

A financial newsletter did a comparison of what two people would have after forty years of saving $50 per month. One person only saved $50 per month for eight years, but let it sit and compound after that for thirty-two years, until she was sixty-five. Her total contribution was $4,800, but at age sixty-five she had $256,650. The other person didn't add any money to his account for the first eight years, then added $50 per month for the next thirty-two years. His total contribution was $22,200, but at age sixty-five he only had $217,830. The moral of the story is, save as soon as you can. It adds up.

Ways to Save

Once you have decided that saving is a good idea, putting that money away can be tricky. It's really tempting to do something else with it. So try these steps to help save:

- Start with a payroll deduction so you never see the money.
- When you finish paying off a loan, take that monthly amount

and put it into the savings account.

- Invest the savings in a low-risk earning account. See the section below on investing.
- Take advantage of your or your spouse's workplace 401K and any matching fund programs.
- Take your spare change at the end of each day and put it in a jar. At the end of each month invest it.
- Stop smoking and put the extra cash in savings.
- Take a sack lunch more often and put the savings in the bank (this savings can range from $60–$100 per month, depending on what you spend for lunch).
- Instead of buying that lottery ticket, put that dollar in the bank (your return will be better).
- Instead of eating out, put that $25 (or more) you would spend into a savings account.

Investing

By investing your money instead of having it sit in a savings account, you may double your money in half the time that it would take in a traditional savings account. You don't have to have much money in order to invest. Nor do you need to be on the phone three times per day to a stockbroker or follow the New York Stock Exchange's daily fluctuations to make some money with investments.

Here are some tips for investing your saved money:

- Decide how much you can invest every month. Make sure your debt is paid off first, since it usually charges more (9–15 percent) than you could earn with an investment (4–8 percent).
- Decide if you want a high- or low-risk investment. A low-risk investment is one that has little risk of losing your initial investment but offers lower returns: balanced mutual funds (small portion of the fund invested in stocks), CDs, savings bonds. High-risk investments offer a higher return (percentage rate) but run a higher risk of losing your investment: stocks, mutual funds invested heavily in the stock market.
- Research the type of investment you are considering (stocks, bonds, real estate) for the pitfalls and strengths.
- Invest the money in a retirement account (401K, IRA). You get

the tax deduction for the deposit and you save for the future.

- Don't put all of your savings in one type of investment—spread it out between stocks, mutual funds, real estate, etc. Even within a retirement account you can vary how your money is invested.
- Save for college using U.S. savings bonds. These defer interest taxation to when used and then only tax on the parents' income, and only if it's over a certain level. For this, buy in the parents' name. If you buy in the student's name and cash in after the child turns fourteen, they are taxed at the child's rate.
- Buy U.S. savings bonds. There is no risk to your investment (they are guaranteed by the federal government), rates adjust every six months to meet inflation, and they are exempt from state and local taxes. To benefit from these, you need a long-term investment (over five years).
- Many mutual funds may waive the large initial investment requirement of $500–$1000 if you agree to a monthly investment amount of $50 or more (there may be a few that will accept payments of $25 per month).
- If investing in mutual funds, only buy no-load mutual funds (a load is a fee just to sign up).
- Don't invest in a mutual fund that focuses on only one market area (e.g., scientific research, Asian markets, gold, etc.). Invest in broader spectrum mutual funds.
- Use a low-cost broker. They often charge 70 percent less than full-service brokers. Some reputable ones include:
  Charles Schwab: (800) 435-4000 *www.schwab.com*
  Fidelity Investments: (800) 544-7272 *www.fidelity.com*
  Quick & Reilly: (800) 793-8050 *www.quickandreilly.com*
- Check out any company that you will invest in. A mutual fund's performance can be researched on Standard and Poor's Fund Services (*www.funds-sp.com*) (also available from your broker).

RESOURCES

Getting Out of Debt and Being Financially Free
Avanzini, John. *Rapid Debt-Reduction Strategies*. His Publishing, 1990.

Blue, Ron. *Taming the Money Monster: Five Steps to Conquering Debt.* Focus on the Family, 1993.

Feinberg, Andrew. *Downsize Your Debt.* Penguin, 1993.

Hammond, Bob. *Life After Debt: How to Repair Your Credit and Get Out of Debt Once and for All.* Career, 1999.

Hunt, Mary. *The Cheapskate Monthly Money Makeover.* St. Martin's Paperbacks, 1995.

Mundis, Jerold. *How to Get Out of Debt, Stay Out of Debt, and Live Prosperously.* Bantam Books, 1990.

Thomsett, Michael C. *How to Get Out of Debt.* Irwin Publishing, 1990.

Budgeting

Burkett, Larry. *Family Budget Workbook: Gaining Control of Your Personal Finances.* Northfield Publishing, 1993.

———. *Larry Burkett's Cash Organizer: Envelope Budgeting System.* Moody, 1995.

Lawrence, Judy. *The Budget Kit: The Common Cent$ Money Management WorkBook.* Dearborn Financial Publishing, 2000.

Longo, Tracey. *10-Minute Guide to Household Budgeting.* Alpha Books, 1997.

McCullough, Bonnie. *Bonnie's Household Budget Book: The Essential Guide for Getting Control of Your Money.* St. Martin's Griffin, 1996.

Peetz, Tuttie. *Basic Budgeting and Money Management: A Guide for Taking Control of Your Spending.* Systems Company, 1997.

Frugal Saving and Investing

Barnes, Bob, and Emilie Barnes. *The 15-Minute Money Manager.* Harvest House, 1993.

Blue, Ron. *Master Your Money.* Thomas Nelson Publishers, 1997.

Burkett, Larry. *The Complete Guide to Managing Your Money.* Budget Book Service, 1996.

———. *The Family Financial Workbook.* Moody, 2000.

———. *Your Complete Guide to Financial Security: How to Invest and Prepare for Your Future Peace of Mind.* Budget Book Service, 1998.

Chilton, David. *The Wealthy Barber: Everyone's Commonsense Guide to Becoming Financially Independent.* Prima Publishing, 1998.

Dunnan, Nancy. *How to Invest $50–$5,000.* Harper Collins, 1999.

Eisenson, Marc. *The Banker's Secret.* Villard Books, 1990.

Moore, Gary. *Ten Golden Rules for Financial Success.* Zondervan Publishing House, 1996.

O'Neill, Barbara. *Saving on a Shoestring: How to Cut Expenses, Reduce Debt, Stash More Cash.* Dearborn, 1994.

Pond, Jonathan D. *The New Century Family Money Book: Your Comprehensive Guide to a Lifetime of Financial Security.* Dell, 1995.

Pryor, Austin. *Sound Mind Investing: A Step-by-Step Guide to Financial Stability and Growth As We Move Toward the Year 2000,* Sound Mind Investing, 2000.

Skousen, Mark. *The New Scrooge Investing: The Bargain Hunter's Guide to Thrifty Investments.* McGraw-Hill, 2000.

Steamer, James. *Wealth on Minimal Wage.* Dearborn Financial Publishing, 1997.

CHAPTER TEN

Moving Right Along: Moving Expenses

The road to a friend's house is never long.

—Danish Proverb

$ $ $

*A*t some point in your life's journey you'll probably be faced with a move. It might be as simple as across town, or perhaps across the country.

We live in a mobile society. The U.S. Census reports that 43.4 million people moved between March 1999 and March 2000.[1] The average person will move eleven times in his life. Chances are that you'll be one of those people.

People move for many reasons. Some move into a college dormitory or when they get married. Often a job transfer or a new job requires relocation. Those families who are serving in the military tend to be moving experts. Some people actually like moving: they enjoy the opportunity to start afresh or to see a new place. Whatever the reason you find yourself moving, here are some ways to make the move easier on you, your family, and your checkbook.

*P*LANNING

Whether moving locally or out of state, the key to a smooth move is organization. Good organization will not only save you time and energy, it will reduce your stress level and save you money. No matter how long or short your move is, the procedure and considerations are basically the same. However, the farther you have to go, the more planning and effort will be required.

Moving begins with pencil and paper, so grab a cup of coffee and spend some time creating a moving notebook. This notebook will become your lifeline during the moving process. There are lots of ways to set up your notebook: it could be done by room, by task, by date, by resource, by person, or by location. A friend of mine recently moved from Colorado to Arizona, and her notebook had sections for both the old home and the new home with to-do lists, inventories, contacts (addresses and phone numbers), and a calendar timeline. Her notebook was a three-ring binder with pocket dividers to insert important documents and mail.

Begin by assessing your housing needs and wants. If you cannot live without it, it is a need. Examples might be a bedroom for each child, a guest room, a garage for your tools, or a yard for the children to play in. Maybe the home needs to be within walking distance of the school or within a certain commuting distance. Consider your entire family's needs. When we moved from the Bay Area to Colorado, I did not want a postage-stamp lot. The kids needed room to play, and I wanted a garden. Additionally, we wanted a bedroom for each child and a home where we could comfortably have guests over. My husband is a bookworm, so "library" space to accommodate all his books was also high on our list. Each family's list will be different. One person's need might be another person's want.

I recommend that people take their time looking for a home. I have heard so many stories of families who had one weekend to buy a house and for years regretted their choice. To avoid that mistake ourselves, we had our belongings stored by the mover for six weeks and rented a furnished apartment. This meant we would only have to unpack once. We had a few suitcases with us for the temporary housing. If we couldn't find a furnished apartment that would allow such a short rental time, we were going to move into a hotel. We did find an apartment and began house hunting. I am so glad we did it this way. It took me three weeks to find the home that fit our needs list. If I hadn't done this, we would have bought something we were not happy with. Not everyone has the time or money to do what I did. Other ways to cut down on house-hunting time are to do the research long distance. With today's technology, the Internet and fax machines make house hunting easier. Have a real estate agent send you information on the neighborhoods as well as actual home listings.

Another important part of the notebook will be a calendar or timeline. You might prefer a blank calendar or a wall calendar to one in your notebook. If you have a specific moving date, start there and work your way backward. Put everything on it from large to small. Items could include specific events like medical appointments or service appointments as well as deadlines to complete certain tasks, such as reserving a moving truck, returning library books, and canceling the newspaper. It might have children's activities on it as well as reminders to do certain things.

Another list for your notebook may be a helper's list. When you tell your friends and family about your upcoming move, often they will offer to help you in some way. Take them up on it! Write down who offered to watch the kids, lift heavy boxes, clean, pack, or bring a meal. When the time comes for one of those tasks, you'll know who offered that help and you'll have the contact information at your fingertips. Make sure you follow up with a thank-you note and/or a small gift of appreciation afterward. When my friend recently moved, she had meals and lodging lined up as well as ladies who helped clean her old place.

Pricing Your Move

Another area to brainstorm is the potential costs involved in your move. Expenses include, but are not limited to, materials for packing, moving vans and equipment rentals, temporary lodging and meals, extra automobile transport, gasoline, house-hunting trips, possibly airline tickets to your new location, storage costs, fees for setting up new utility services, and the list goes on. List all your potential costs and how you plan to meet them. Perhaps you'll need some of the proceeds from the sale of your old home or the security deposit from your rental to pay for the move. While there are ways to reduce these costs, which I will discuss later, the bottom line is this: moving costs money. Even if your employer pays for the relocation, the move still costs money. So before you decide to leave the snow-packed mountains with sub-zero temperatures for the warm beach, count the cost and make sure you can afford to do so. Starting a new adventure in a new place in debt is not the way to go.

$$ TIP:

Keep accurate records of your moving expenses, since they might be tax-deductible. Check out what qualifies as a tax-deductible expense by ordering IRS publication 521 entitled "Moving Expenses." Contact the IRS at (800) 829-3676 or on the Web at *www.irs.gov*.

You may not have a choice on when you move, but if you do, here are some things to consider. Just as with hotels and vacation destinations, there are peak and off-peak times for moving. These can affect the price and availability of the movers and trucks. According to the American Movers Conference, interstate moving companies are the busiest during the summer months, with 45 percent[2] of moves occurring during that time. For local moves, weekends are busier than weekdays. Another good reason to avoid moving over a weekend is that most utility services are closed on weekends. Resolving any problems that might occur will be nearly impossible. Wouldn't it be awful to bring all your food from your old home to your new one and discover you have no refrigerator for two days because the electricity wasn't turned on?

How Much Stuff Do I Have?

Probably one of the more extensive projects in planning your move is to calculate the amount of stuff you have to move. Whether you are going to do it yourself or hire someone to move it for you, you need to know the approximate cubic feet of possessions you'll be moving. This will determine the size truck or the amount of space in a moving van you'll need. The following guidelines can give you a rough idea of how to estimate this. It's probably a good idea to err on the high side if you are unsure. Most moving companies will estimate this for you as part of their bid, but it's still a good exercise for you to inventory your household.

- Small boxes = 3 cubic feet
- Large boxes = 6 cubic feet
- Beds and large appliances = 30–40 cubic feet
- Couches and buffets = 30 cubic feet
- Recliners, medium appliances, such as washers/dryers = 20 cubic feet
- TVs, chests, tables = 10 cubic feet
- Six-foot wide closets = 30–40 cubic feet

Weight is the second component in determining the cost of your move. If you plan to hire a moving company, you'll be charged by the weight of your shipment. On average, each box or piece of furniture in your shipment weighs 35–45 pounds. This should give you a rough estimate of the net weight of your possessions.

Decluttering Family Treasures

Doing the inventory serves a dual purpose. Not only will it help you project your moving costs and determine what equipment you'll need, but it is also an excellent opportunity to take stock of what you have and make some decisions about whether all the things you own will be moving with you. The longer you have been in one place, the more decluttering there is to be done. So . . . plan a garage sale or two! After all, the less stuff you move, the less money you'll spend to move it, not to mention the effort. And you could make money from the sale or get a tax write-off for donating items to a charity (get a receipt!).

So how does one tackle the process of weeding through the family treasures? How much time you have to make the move will probably determine how in depth you can go. Make four categories: move it, sell it, give it away, and throw it away. A general rule of thumb: if you haven't used it or worn it in the past year, it's probably not worth moving. How about those boxes you never unpacked from the last time you moved? If you haven't used them since then, do you need to pay to move them again?

Another consideration is heavy items. Take your son's weight set. Let's say you did the math and figured out it was going to cost you $1 to move every pound of stuff. Is it worth $120 to move your son's $60 weight set? Maybe sell or donate it and purchase a new one once you get to your destination. Canned goods are other items you might want to consider donating and purchasing again in your new location. My friends decided to sell their ten-year-old washer and dryer rather than move them, since they were old and would cost more to move than they were worth. Another consideration is your furniture. Will all of it fit into your new house? If not, don't pay to move it!

Now that you have decluttered and have a reasonable estimate of the weight and cubic feet of the items to be moved, you need to know the distance from your old home to your new one. If you are hiring a moving company, they will determine this for you. All they need are starting and ending addresses. If, however, you are moving yourself, here are some key tips to remember:

- The shortest route might not be the best route. The more weight in the truck, the harder time you'll have over mountain passes or across hot deserts.
- Take weather and road conditions into consideration when planning the route.
- Check to see if there is major construction on the highway you are thinking about using. Visit the National Traffic and Road Closure Web site (*http://www.fhwa.dot.gov/trafficinfo*) provided by the United States Department of Transportation—Federal Highway Administration.
- Keep in mind that you'll be going slower and shorter distances per day if you choose to drive a rental truck. Plan on about four hundred miles per day in a rental truck and up to five hundred miles per day if driving a car. Of course, those numbers might be lower if you have young children, pets, or are just not a long-distance driver.

$\mathcal{D}$O IT MYSELF OR MOVING COMPANY?

This is the million-dollar question. There are pros and cons to both choices. Having someone come in, pack up your belongings, drive them to your new location, and unpack them for you is very convenient. Doing it yourself may not be practical if you are moving from Connecticut to Oregon. If your employer is paying for all or part of the move, then you may be able to make some convenient choices. However, if you are paying for this move yourself, doing it yourself may be better. Who's paying and other considerations discussed below will help you make this decision.

Let's start with doing it yourself. A big factor will be the distance you have to travel. If your move is a short distance, you may be able to do most or all of it by recruiting friends with trucks, trailers, and minivans. This is a relatively inexpensive route. Or you may want to move the boxes and smaller items with friends but hire a professional to move the large furniture and appliances.

If you choose to rent a moving truck, do your homework first. There is more to consider than just the price of the truck or trailer rental. Can you reserve a specific truck for the day you need it? Some rental places don't guarantee the truck you want will be available. Is it rented by the twenty-four-hour day or by the eight-hour day? Do you need a tow bar or auto carrier for your vehicle? Are there any drop-off charges? Find out what equipment—such as dollies and furniture pads—is included in the price and how much additional items cost. Check with your insurance company about what is covered and what is not in terms of contents and driver. Many rental places offer, and some require, supplemental insurance at a cost to you. Other cost-related questions include the fuel efficiency (miles per gallon) for the loaded vehicle: they usually get seven miles to the gallon when loaded.

Other logistical questions include: Does the vehicle have an automatic or manual transmission? How old is it? Is it air-conditioned? How many passengers can it hold? What type of gasoline does it take? If possible, inspect the vehicle before you rent it. Does the truck have a spare tire and emergency

What Size Truck Do You Need?

14-foot truck = 750 cubic feet = avg. 2-bedroom apartment

18-foot truck = 1,000 cubic feet = avg. 2-bedroom house

24-foot truck = 1,400 cubic feet = avg. 3-bedroom house

A professional 40-foot van holds 4,000 cubic feet.

flares? Does the truck have a ramp or hydraulic lift? Can you pick it up the night before? How many days and miles are included in the price? If I exceed the allotment, how much will it cost?

A very important issue to understand is the procedure if the vehicle breaks down. Make sure you have, in writing, who is responsible for the breakdown, how long you will have to wait for help, who pays for any hotel or food if you have to wait, and where it must be taken to get repaired. I have friends who rented a moving truck, and several hundred miles into their trip they noticed an oil leak. It turned out the truck had a broken oil gasket. It cost them two travel days waiting for it to be fixed. After they set off again, they discovered the repair hadn't worked. They resolved to stop every seventy-five miles to put fresh oil in the vehicle so they could arrive on time to sign the closing papers on their new house. The rental company did reimburse them for the repairs and oil and even for the extra meals and lodging.

Moving Companies

Perhaps your employer will pay for a moving company to move your household. Or perhaps your move is across the country and the thought of riding in a rental truck for several days is not that appealing. Even if your employer is not paying for relocation, it doesn't hurt to research this option for long-distance moves. Begin by obtaining a minimum of three estimates from different companies. Ask friends, neighbors (especially those who have recently moved), or maybe even your employer for recommendations of companies they have used and what kind of service they received. Check with the Better Business Bureau on the company that you pick (*www.bbb.org*).

Before the company representative even comes out to give an estimate (if they charge for this, move on—plenty of companies do it for free), ask how long they have been in business and the experience of their packers and drivers. If you know you'll need storage, make sure the company offers it. And make sure the company is licensed and regulated.

During the interview with the moving company representative, ask lots of questions. Find out exactly what services are offered. What insurance coverage do they offer? Does it cover only items the company packs or will it cover items packed by the owner? If they will be packing your goods, is the crew bonded? What is their on-time arrival percentage? Can you call and locate your goods at any time? Are there any guarantees? What discounts might you qualify for? Sometimes senior citizens and government or military personnel receive discounts. Ask if there is a discount to move during an off-peak time. The company should allow you to visit their office and storage facilities. By law you are allowed to be present when the truck is weighed, so be wary if they tell you otherwise.

Moving companies generally offer two kinds of contracts. A binding contract means you will not be required to pay more than the estimate. Legally, the binding estimate must be in writing, describing the details of the shipment including dates, addresses, and inventory of goods. Make sure you have a copy of it before you move. Some companies charge for a binding estimate. Of course, if you require services above and beyond the original estimate, the company is allowed to charge for those items.

Savings Tips
- Move Monday to Thursdays
- Move in the middle of a month
- Avoid the summer months

Compare estimates before signing an agreement. My friend discovered that estimating cubic feet is not an exact science. She received four bids, and the estimated weight based on cubic footage varied by 3,500 pounds between the four bids!

The second type of contract a moving company offers is a non-binding estimate. Often there is no charge for this. As with a binding contract, the estimate must be in writing and detail the shipment, but there is no guarantee of the final cost. The moving company will give you an estimated cost, but the final cost will be based on the actual weight of your shipment. Legally, you cannot be held responsible for more than 10 percent above the original estimate. But, as with the binding estimate, any additional services that you asked for that were not a part of the original estimate can be charged to you.

The bottom line on estimates is this: make sure you know and understand exactly what kind of estimate you have and what is and is not included in that estimate.

Additional insurance is another option to consider in your moving contract. Don't assume that all damage will be covered!

Your homeowner's insurance will probably not cover your goods, since they are usually covered for fire or theft, not damage by movers. Additional coverage will cost you, depending on the company and the items being insured. But it's worth the investment. If you only take the standard "released value" insurance that is included with your move, you get reimbursed for 60¢ per pound of loss. Hence, if the contents of your three-bedroom apartment, weighing 3,456 pounds, were destroyed or lost, you would only get $2,100 in damages. And some of the self-service movers only reimburse you 10¢ per pound. With them, the "free" insurance would only get you $345 in damages. Look into the declared value, lump sum value, and full value protection insurance options for your goods. The full replacement value can cost you $8.50 for every $1,000 of declared value. Subsequently, if your goods are valued at $10,000, you will pay $85 for the added protection. It's well worth it!

Once you've narrowed the field to a couple of choices, verify if your mover is a member of a trade organization such as the American Movers Conference (*www.amconf.org*). Membership is not required, but those who choose to be members are serious about their industry. Their membership also gives you, the consumer, another contact should there be grievances regarding your move. Also check with the Better Business Bureau (*www.bbb.org*) to see if any complaints have been lodged against the company you are considering.

There is a third type of moving company that I should mention. Some movers offer the truck and driver only. They do not offer packing, loading the truck, or unloading. This may be a happy medium for many families who don't want the hassle of dealing with a rental truck that they have to drive or that may break down. And it saves them money by doing the packing and loading themselves. Some examples of a company like this are MoveX (*www.movex.com*), Help-U-Move (*www.helpumove.com*), Move America (*www.moveamerica.com*), and CF Moves U (*www.cfmovesu.com*). Make sure that the Federal Motor Carrier Safety Administration (FMCSA) has licensed the company for the transporting of household goods across state lines, by asking for their USDOT MC number (United States Dept. of Transportation

Motor Carrier number), or check with the FMCSA at *http://fmcsa.dot.gov.*

Cost Comparison

Here are some estimated bids on moving the contents of a three-bedroom house halfway across the U.S. As you can see, letting a mover load and drive for you may be the cheapest way.

Do-It-Yourself Rental Truck		$2,500–3,000
Truck	$1,500	
Extra expenses: gas (at 7 miles per gallon), extra hotels and meals because you can't drive as far each day, lost time off work for the extra days, physical therapy after you are done, and packing materials	$1,000–1,500	
Full Service Mover		$5,000
Includes packing materials, packing, loading, and unloading		
Partial Service Mover		$2,500
Includes loading, driving, and unloading		
Self-Service Movers		$2,000
You pack, you load, they drive, you unload	$1,500	
Packing materials	$ 500	

Some great sites for calculating your moving costs are:

www.imove.com/Moving/default.asp (calculates moving expenses)
www.homefair.com/ (looks at salary and cost-of-living changes, calculates moving expenses)

PACKING

Packing things yourself can save you a bundle of money. For example, to pack one small standard moving box cost a friend $24 to have the moving crew do it. She did it herself for under $5. Price that out over a whole house and the savings are tremendous. If you have the mover pack everything, you might receive a better rate than this.

Moving is stressful. It ranks third behind death and divorce as the most stressful factors in life. Plan time out every day to do something you like—take a bath, read a book, do lunch, visit with a friend.

Besides the convenience, there are some additional advantages to having a professional packing crew do your packing. They have knowledge and experience as well as the equipment to do the job. They will do it far more quickly than you can do it. A friend of mine did most of the packing herself but ran out of time. She had a packing crew come in to finish the kitchen and a few other items. Within two hours two men had the whole thing done. Another reason to have movers pack for you is that they will insure those items. Boxes packed by you might not be covered. Check their policy before packing. One tip my friend passed on was to watch how they bill for this. Since this crew came at the end of the day, they had run short of boxes. My friend still had plenty of boxes she had purchased, and the crew used them. On the final inventory sheet, however, the crew marked that they had provided the boxes and were going to charge her as such. My watchful friend caught the error and had it corrected. Catching that error saved her several hundred dollars.

The professional moving crew has no emotional investment in the job they are doing. The moving crew doesn't know the difference between an ordinary vase and the one your great grandmother brought from Sweden a century ago. In fact, it is advisable to pack anything of value (sentimental or otherwise) yourself. It seems to be a given that no move will go perfectly. I have heard this same story from other friends who have moved with different companies.

Items of importance to you should not only be packed by you but also be transported in your car if possible. Anything that could be devastating to lose should be considered valuable. These might include jewelry, silver utensils, heirlooms, tax forms, insurance information, business receipts, medical records, photographs, school records, computer files, etc. Additionally, movers may not insure some of these items, even if they pack them.

Once you have decided what you will pack, the next issue is whether to use a hodge-podge of free boxes or to purchase moving boxes from a moving supply store. Certainly there is a cost difference. I think the answer depends on the type of move you are making. Most damage occurs when things move around inside the box. Moving boxes are strong and sturdy, more so than grocery store boxes. Since moving boxes are uniform in shape, you can pack the vehicle tightly to minimize space and movement. Packing the vehicle with many odd-shaped boxes will make it more difficult, take longer, and probably use more space than if all the boxes are uniform. Now, if you are using your own vehicles and moving locally, it might take more trips but be worth it to use the mix-and-match approach to boxes. Good sources for free boxes are grocery stores, office supply stores, paint stores, furniture stores, appliance stores, and bookstores. Also look in the Yellow Pages for used-box stores. Often you can purchase used moving boxes at a fraction of the cost of new ones. One friend was able to purchase gently used moving boxes for $1–$3 a box depending on the size and type.

Packing materials are another area for potential savings. Newspaper is cheap and works for packing, but the ink will rub off

Use small boxes for heavy items and large boxes for lighter items.

on your hands, clothes, and items in your box. Clean wrapping paper can be purchased at most moving stores and is probably a wise investment, especially for your dishes. If you have any left over, it makes great drawing paper for the kids. It is also recyclable. Don't forget about using towels, blankets, linens, and clothes. Nestling breakable items in the middle of a blanket will provide additional cushioning and is free.

Common sense helps in packing items too. Unpacking will be easier if you pack items from the same room in the same box. Wrap fragile hard items with soft items. Don't overload the boxes. They should be easy to carry. Make sure they are packed well, stuffing empty spaces with packing material or newspaper. If things move around when you gently shake the box, imagine the damage that can be done while they are being loaded and transported to your new home. The few cents for extra packing paper is worth it in the long run. Seal boxes well with tape as opposed to just folding in the top flaps. Overstuffed boxes can burst and underfilled boxes can be easily crushed.

Sketch or take a Polaroid picture of stereo and computer equipment wiring before disconnecting. This will save time and frustration in setting them up again in your new home. Store in your notebook.

Assigning each box a code helps with organization: G can stand for garage, K for kitchen, LR for living room, etc. Each box can also receive a number. On paper write the corresponding number and a list of what is in the box. This list serves a dual purpose. If a box were lost in the move, you would know exactly what items to claim for insurance purposes. It also helps increase the efficiency in organizing your new home with boxes easily being identified and put in their correct rooms. Local moves don't require near as much effort in packing since the distance is shorter.

Loading the Vehicle

There are some tricks of the trade in loading your vehicle. Done properly it can save you money in two ways. First, if you load the truck properly, all items should fit tightly. Loose loading makes for wasted space and an opportunity for jostling items. We had friends who did not pack things well and had to rent an additional trailer to hitch onto the rental truck to accommodate all their items. This was money they had not planned on spending.

Second, a well-packed truck will minimize damage and breakage. When loading the truck, have one person organizing the load while other workers take items to him. Load items to form squares and rectangles, placing heavy items on the bottom, working floor to ceiling. There should be little or no space between boxes. Small boxes can fit under chairs. To protect your furniture and appliances, wrap them in furniture pads.

An unbalanced trailer or truck can be dangerous to the driver and to a vehicle being towed. Distribute weight evenly, placing the washer and dryer on one side and the refrigerator on the other side. Load heavy items toward the front and over the axles. If your truck has an attic, place electronics and fragile items there. Save the lightweight and odd-shaped items for the top of the load. And last but not least: items you need first, load last.

Special Equipment

A few pieces of equipment that are available for rent can greatly reduce time and risk of injury. One of these is a dolly. There are three types of dollies:

Consider hiring a professional to move pianos since they are so delicate and heavy. And remember to tune a piano after you move it.

- An appliance dolly is five feet or taller with a cinch strap. It can carry five hundred pounds or more. Use this to move washers, dryers, and refrigerators.
- A stock dolly or a hand truck is shorter, three to five feet in height, without a strap. Loading three to four boxes on it makes efficient use of time in loading the truck. Young people can learn to correctly operate this kind of dolly and become big helpers.
- A piano dolly is a 30-by-30-inch square on wheels. It is a must for moving pianos but also works great for large (and heavy) furniture items. When carrying or moving large items, tip them and move the low end out the door first. Consider renting one or more of these dollies to facilitate your move.

Things NOT to Move

If you have hired a moving company, they will provide you with a list of items they cannot move. Items that are prohibited include but are not restricted to: aerosol cans, ammunition, bleach, car batteries, cleaning products, gasoline, other automotive fluids, insecticides, kerosene, lighter fluid, propane tanks, matches, oil-based paints, oxygen tanks, paint thinners, strippers, and turpentine. They also refuse to transport inert items that are opened, such as laundry detergent, floor polish, and shampoo. It may seem a waste to you to toss these items or donate them to friends, but there are good reasons for these rules. A moving truck driver once told the story of a family that decided at the last minute to pack some forbidden cleaning supplies and hairsprays unbeknown to the driver. This box of items, worth maybe $20, was placed over the wheel wells where the brakes can get hot. That box ignited, costing that family all they owned plus three other families all their possessions and $180,000 worth of damage to the truck. Fortunately no one was hurt, but obviously the rules exist to protect you and the driver.

Moving Day

If possible, make arrangements for children and pets to be cared for on this day. It will help you keep your sanity, and they will probably have more fun. If you hired a moving company, plan on being there, out of the way but not out of sight. Check the accuracy of the mover's inventory and any notes of damage. Clearly mark what is to go and what is not. Consider moving items that are not to be touched by the movers to a closet and closing the door. Be clear, because movers will pack trash, draperies, and anything else they see unless you tell them otherwise. Do a final walkthrough before the movers leave to make sure nothing was left behind. If you are doing the move yourself, picking up the moving vehicle the night before will make the day go faster.

Of course, the final step is cleaning. Consider hiring out for this or enlisting friends to help. I have participated in more than one cleaning party where several women brought their own supplies and quickly cleaned a vacant home. It was fun and a huge help to the person moving.

Moving-In Day and Unpacking

Before the moving truck arrives at your new place, explore your empty house. Make decisions about possible furniture placement. Plan where you want boxes stacked in each room. It's also a good idea to equip at least one bathroom with toilet paper, soap, towels, and shower curtain. Having disposable cups for water or other drinks helps too. Through much experience, I've learned that making up the beds receives top priority. Check your inventory sheet for the location of those bed linens. At the end of your moving-in day you'll be happy to fall into the freshly made bed.

Which rooms get set up first is entirely up to you. After a place to sleep and a functional bathroom, I find it a toss-up between setting up the kitchen or the kids' rooms. One book I read suggested setting up the living room first so the children could watch TV or videos. Children like routine and familiar surroundings, so I tend to set up their rooms first. Often they'll play for hours with newly discovered toys they haven't seen for a while. The kitchen is next on my list so we can have home-cooked meals again as soon as possible. It also contributes to a sense of routine. We'll discuss this more in "The Emotional Side of Moving."

Disputes With Movers

Hopefully this won't be your experience, but if your possessions were damaged in the move, you have some recourse. First, make sure you know what you are insured for! As mentioned earlier, being underinsured can become more costly than the additional insurance. Every moving company has a complaint and inquiry process. Move up the chain of command, remembering to be polite and professional. You have nine months from the delivery date to file a claim with the mover (they will send you the forms upon request). The company in turn must acknowledge your claim within thirty days and resolve or deny your claim within 120 days.

If your claim is denied or the settlement is not to your satisfaction, try contacting the American Movers Conference Dispute Settlement Program (*www.Amconf.org*). You will need the name of the mover, identification number of the shipment, dates and locations of pickup and delivery, and estimated value of loss. With arbitration there will be forms to complete as well as fees in the neighborhood of $150. You may also contact the American Arbitration Association (*www.adr.org*).

THE EMOTIONAL SIDE OF MOVING

Getting your belongings to your new home is only half of the moving experience. The list of changes your family may experience can include job, work hours and/or conditions, schools, churches, organizational affiliations, recreational settings, social activities, proximity to friends and family, finances, and leaving pets and/or friends. Each one can be stressful and is an adjustment for each family member. Often how smooth a move goes depends on your attitude about the move. Try to be as positive as you can about it, especially when you don't have a choice. Focus on the adventure of exploring a new place, making new friends, having new opportunities, new shopping, new neighbors, and the development of new habits or a fresh start.

If your move is not local, research your new area. Try the bookstore or library for books and newspapers about your new locale. We subscribed to the local newspaper before we moved so we could become familiar with the city. The Internet can provide a wealth of information about a new area. One company, Location Guides, has put together one-hundred-page guides for about two hundred cities that include information and contacts on local, state, and regional levels. Check out their Web site at *www.locationguides.com*. If you are a member of AAA, see what information it can provide. Contact the state Chamber of Commerce for an official state handbook. It will include government, political, social, and historical information including useful phone numbers. Even a tourism brochure will provide some information.

> Kids will focus on the loss of their room, home, and friends. Teens will focus on emotions. Adults focus on physical details.

The emotional side begins as early as telling your family about the move. Children don't like change and may have a negative reaction at first. Tell them of the upcoming move as soon as possible so they'll have time to prepare and adjust. Break it to them gently, tailoring the discussion for their age. Don't overburden children with too many details, but give solid reasons for the move. Be prepared to answer their questions and to tell them (or show them if you can) about the new location. Remain positive without sugar-coating it. Communicate understanding of their emotions. Decide when to make the announcement public.

The entire process can be an emotional roller coaster for all family members, but especially for children. Be patient and a good listener. Deal with all misconceptions immediately. One child I knew feared that moving meant leaving all her toys and bed behind. Reassure children, especially younger ones, that all their favorite toys and bed will be going with them. Additionally, involve the children where appropriate. Maybe allow a child to help pack a box of his things. One child I knew had to say good-bye to each stuffed animal as it was packed. Even though you have a lot to do, make time for your children no matter how old they are. It's tough on them too. Our friends who were relocating for a job were allowed only one house-hunting trip—for the parents only. This couple took their video camera and videotaped the area and the entire new house for their daughter to see before she ever set foot in it.

So how long does it take to adjust to your new surroundings? Researchers estimate it takes one to three years to sink roots down into a new community. Be prepared for it to take a while for your new home to feel like home. Making new friends takes effort. Whether it's your personality or not, you need to become the initiator. Take a plate of cookies to your neighbor and introduce yourself. (Or if someone has just moved into your neighborhood, do that for her.) Become involved in school or community activities. Find a church and invite people to your home for a meal. Explore your new town, ask questions of your neighbors about what places or events they enjoy or recommend. Volunteering is also a great way to meet new people. Seek out places and activities for your children to make friends too. The faster they feel they are in a routine, the better and quicker their adjustment will be. It takes time, but don't lose heart; soon your new home will be filled with memories. Remember to cherish the old, not cling to it. I've included several books on the next page to help you with the emotional side of moving. I hope they will help your move be a positive experience.

RESOURCES

Banks, Ann. *Good-bye, House: A Kids Guide to Moving.* Crown Publishing, 1999.

Carlisle, Ellen. *Smooth Moves.* Teacup Press, 1999.

Davis, Gabriel. *The Moving Book: A Kid's Survival Guide.* Little Brown & Co, 1997.

Goodwin, Cathy. *Making the Big Move: How to Transform Relocation Into a Creative Life Transition.* New Harbinger Publications, 1999.

Levine, Leslie. *Will This Place Ever Feel Like Home: Simple Advice for Settling in After Your Move.* Dearborn Publishing, 1998.

Miller, Susan. *After the Boxes Are Unpacked: Moving On After Moving In.* Focus on the Family, 1998.

Steiner, Clyde, and Shari Steiner. *Steiner's Complete How-to-Move Handbook.* Dell, 1996.

CHAPTER ELEVEN

Insurance

Don't go to a doctor whose plants have died.

—Erma Bombeck

HOMEOWNER'S AND RENTER'S INSURANCE

Whether you are a renter or a homeowner, you should have protection for your goods. If you own your home, protecting the home is essential as well. The loss of your goods or home is devastating. There are so many ways that our homes and/or belongings can be damaged. We should try to get a policy that covers all of our needs—inexpensively. We also need to make sure that we are covered for what we believe we are paying for.

Aside from protecting the building and contents, a homeowner's or renter's policy provides other coverage you may be surprised about. For the extras, see "Coverage You Didn't Know You Had" later in the chapter.

Make sure you have adequate coverage for these basic areas:

Homeowner's Insurance for the Dwelling

This is the building that you live in, with any attached buildings, such as a garage. You should be mainly concerned about the cost of rebuilding your home. To find out exactly what you need, learn what the average cost is to build in your area (per square foot). This can be found by contacting a local builder's association. Multiply this figure by the square feet in your home, and insure for that amount.

Make sure that you have replacement value coverage. This means that as the cost of rebuilding rises over time, your policy will still cover the full cost of the repair. Without this coverage, the insurance company could say that you will only get a percentage of the value. Consumer groups do not recommend insuring for market value. That coverage usually includes your land and may not cover the rebuilding costs.

Make sure that you are covered for what it will actually cost to replace the items in your home as well as the building. Many policies cover a depreciated value and not the cost of replacement.

If you live in a townhouse or condominium, ask the homeowner's association to clarify what part of the building structure is your responsibility. Also ask what portion, if any, of the grounds is your responsibility. Some yards are the responsibility of the association, while others are the responsibility of the homeowner.

Other Structures on Your Property

This includes anything other than the home and garage. A woodworking shop or greenhouse would be in this category.

Old Buildings Coverage

This is not the actual name of the coverage type, but it gets the point across. If you have an older building that could have defects in it from age, a building inspector could order it demolished for safety reasons. The cost of the demolition and rebuilding won't be fully covered by your regular policy. An extended coverage will take care of any gaps.

Loss of Use of Your Dwelling

This provides coverage for expenses you incur while the building is unlivable. These expenses may be the motel you need to live in for a few weeks (or months) while repairs are being done or the meals you need to buy at a restaurant while the kitchen is rebuilt after a grease fire. This coverage is usually included in both homeowner's and renter's policies.

Out-of-the-Ordinary Coverages

Whether you are a homeowner or a renter, you may need protection for belongings or situations that are out of the ordinary. Some things to check for are:

Home Office

If you have an office at home, most policies only cover $2,500 of damage to the equipment. Since most computers and other gadgets used in the home office amount to more than that, you may want to purchase extra coverage.

Earthquake Policy

Having grown up in earthquake country and having lived through some real shakers, I advise anyone living near a fault line to make sure to purchase earthquake coverage. It is an extra financial burden but well worth it when everything literally comes crashing in on you.

After the big California earthquake in 1989, we saw so many homeowners who had no home left but had to continue paying the mortgage. Then they had to pay for the new loan to rebuild the home. Many foreclosed or sold at a loss. An earthquake policy would have prevented that loss.

Flood Insurance

A shocking 90 percent of flood victims are not covered for their damage. Most general policies do not carry flood insurance. It is an extra coverage that carries a surcharge. If you live anywhere near a flood zone, make sure you get the coverage you need. If you cannot get flood coverage (many insurance providers don't offer it), check into the federally administered insurance program offered by FEMA (Federal Emergency Management Agency) or call 888-CALL-FLOOD or check out *www.fema.gov/ nfip/cost1.htm.* You will be referred to an agent in your area who will offer you flood insurance.

Personal Valuables

If you have treasured antiques or valuable jewelry, you may need to purchase additional coverage for those items under your homeowner's policy. Many policies pay a maximum amount for jewelry in case of theft or loss, and it doesn't usually replace much.

Odd Things to Check For

Some policies cover more extras than others. If some of the things in this list are of concern to you, you may need extra coverage for them. A few items to check for are:

- falling objects
- the weight of snow or ice causing damage
- water damage from appliances
- damage from any appliance
- freezing damage to pipes and water systems
- electrical malfunctions that cause damage

Renter's Insurance

When renting a home, you will want to make sure your possessions in the home are adequately insured. The owner is only responsible for the structure and the grounds. You are responsible to insure your belongings inside the home. If you own a waterbed, make sure your insurance covers you for this. Sometimes that requires an extra rider. Also make sure you are covered for loss of use of your home in case a calamity strikes.

Mobile Home Insurance

Mobile home owners often have the headaches of both a renter and a homeowner. They are renters in the sense that frequently the land is not theirs and they pay rent to use the association property and amenities, but they are homeowners because they have the responsibility of the mobile home. Make sure you are covered for the loss of the mobile home itself if damaged and for loss of use. Be sure you are covered for damage if the unit is moved.

Some lenders will require a policy that protects them. Since the home can be moved but it is also the collateral for the loan, you are a higher risk than the owner of a stationary home. This protects the lien holder if you skip town with the home.

Limits of Liability

Most policies limit what they will pay for certain categories. Here are a few examples:

- Lost cash—$200
- Securities, bank notes, tickets, stamp collections, etc.—$1,000
- Jewelry—$1,000
- Firearms—$2,000
- Silverware—$2,500
- Office equipment—$2,500
- Personal property at another location—$250

Not Covered

Some things will not be covered under any policy. Sometimes a rider can be purchased separately for some of these. Here are some common exclusions:

- Sinkholes
- Freeze damage to a vacant dwelling
- Vandalism to a vacant dwelling
- Repeated water damage by an appliance
- Water damage from floods, backed up sewers, leaking swimming pools, underground streams
- Power failures (that are area wide)
- Neglect
- Earth movement (quakes or slides)
- War
- Nuclear incident
- Decision made by local government
- Pets
- Motor vehicles damaged in a fire or calamity to the home
- Watercrafts, snowmobiles, all-terrain vehicles, Jet Skis, hang gliders
- Property of tenants
- Bookkeeping material

- Intentional acts by you (such as punching someone)
- Damages caused by business activity on the property
- Defective or decaying material
- Damages caused by a vehicle to the building

How to Keep Costs Down

Shop Around

Premiums are not the same at every company, even for the same locations. Rates can vary $200 or more per year.

Keep a High Deductible

The minimum deductible is usually $250 on a homeowner's policy. By raising that to $500 or $1,000, you can deduct up to 25 percent off your annual premiums. Remember that insurance is to help pay for things our savings cannot cover.

Don't Over- or Underinsure

Get a policy that covers only your needs. Don't try to get rich off of your calamities by having inflated coverage.

Investigate Discounts

Ask your agent if you get discounts for fire detectors, alarm systems, dead bolts, fire extinguishers, multi-policies (having auto and home with the same carrier), nonsmoker household, long-term customer, mature residents with no children, retirees, or fire-resistant roofing material. These are just a few areas to ask about. Some of these conditions offer as much as a 25 percent discount on the premium.

Don't Skip Around

Jumping from carrier to carrier will eventually catch up with you. Staying with one carrier will offer you a history with them that may lead to a discount.

Coverage You Didn't Know You Had

Many people have some extra coverage provided by their homeowner's policy that they may not know about. Here are a few examples:

- Debris removal caused by a natural disaster, such as a fallen tree or collapsed wall from high wind
- Trees or shrubs lost to natural causes (high winds, freezing, etc.)
- Fees for fire protection services in a rural area
- Check forgery or credit card fraud up to a certain limit
- Loss of luggage or wallet
- If your child throws a ball and breaks a neighbor's window, your insurance will probably pay for it
- Some policies even pay legal fees (but not damages) if you are sued for slander, false arrest, wrongful eviction, or invasion of privacy
- Sometimes even damaged carpeting from spilled bleach is covered.

A note of caution: Many of these items may not be worth claiming. You need to weigh the cost of the damage over the possibility of being categorized as a high-risk customer and thus paying higher premiums in the future—or even having your insurance cancelled.

$\mathcal{C}$AR INSURANCE

Car insurance is a topic that often generates anger and frustration. It is required to legally drive, but many feel it is filled with excessive fees and pricing mysteries. Sometimes we are buying coverage we do not need, and other times we are driving on thin ice.

What We Pay For

Understanding what our policy prices are based on sometimes helps us to know how to shop better for coverage. Here are the basics of how insurance prices are calculated:

Location

Where you live determines what the rate will be. Your state, city, and neighborhood determine the base rate that you will pay. Insurance companies have determined that most accidents occur within a few miles of our homes, so they figure your likelihood of having an accident based on where you live.

Age

Your age tells the insurance companies statistically how mature you might be, and therefore how responsible you should be. Drivers under twenty-five and over sixty-five pay a higher rate than other ages.

Gender

Young single men are statistically worse drivers and will pay a higher rate than women of the same age.

Marital Status

Statistically, a married person tends to be more responsible and will have lower rates than a single person of the same age. You might be able to keep your married person's discount after a divorce if you have custody of one or more children. It's worth asking.

Use of the Car

The primary reasons you drive the car will affect the rate you pay. A pleasure car costs less to insure than a car used for business or for commuting to work. The number of miles you drive each year determines the rate as well.

Type of Car

The type of car you drive also determines the insurance premium you pay. You will pay a higher premium for a four-wheel-drive or recreation vehicle than a minivan. Also, the cost of the car determines the rate. A Mercedes-Benz will cost more to repair than a less expensive vehicle. If a vehicle is known for its safety features, it may cost less to drive. And a car's age and ease of obtaining repair parts also affect the rate.

Driving Record

Your driving record will also determine how much you pay. Each moving violation warns the insurance agency that you are a risky driver, and it will charge you for that extra risk. This can be seen as a generally higher rate or as a surcharge that stays on the policy for three years.

How to Save on Auto Insurance

Deductibles

If you pay a higher deductible, your rate will go down. This means that you are willing to assume a greater share of the damages when they happen. Insurance companies like this.

Lower the Coverage

By changing to the minimum coverage allowed, you can reduce your premiums. Make sure you are covered sufficiently for an accident (medical, time off work, car repairs, etc.), but take no more than that.

Reduce Collision and Comprehensive

If you have a newer car, repairing a scratch or dent will be costly, and you need the comprehensive and collision coverage. If, however, your car is older (five to ten years old), repairing the same will cost less. Lowering your comprehensive coverage will save you in cases like this.

Omit the Extras

Some coverage categories are not required, and avoiding them saves you money. The roadside services coverage is not necessary, especially if you are a member of a travel club like AAA. See if you can do without it. Some consumer groups do not, however, recommend dropping uninsured motorist coverage or liability coverage.

Shop Around

Not all agencies charge the same rates for the same neighborhood. One company considered my neighborhood a high-rate area. Another considered it a good neighborhood and offered lower rates for the same coverage.

Driving Style

Improve your driving record and your rates will go down. It may take a few years to get rid of a violation, but staying alert and driving safely will bring it down.

Buy the Right Car

When buying a car, keep in mind the insurance you will have to pay on it. Call the insurance company before you buy a car and ask which models have the lower rates.

Look for Discounts

There are a number of discounts that will reduce your premium.

- Multi-car discount: Having both cars insured with the same company will give you a discount on both cars.
- Other policies: If you have other policies (home, life, medical) with the same company, you will receive a discount on all of the policies.
- Nonsmoking: Nonsmokers are sometimes offered a better deal.
- Antitheft devices: If you install antitheft devices you will lower your rates.
- Airbags: Some companies offer a discount if you have an airbag installed.
- Good driver discount: If you have a clean driving record, you can get a discount on the car you drive.
- Good student discount: If a younger driver (under age twenty-five) is on your policy, his or her good grades may lower the premiums.
- Middle-age discount: If you are between the ages of fifty and sixty-five you may be offered a lower rate.
- Low mileage: If you drive very few miles each year, you may get a discount.

Coverage You May Not Know You Have

Did you know that there are ways to cover life's blunders? We found out about an unusual way to pay for some damage done to a relative's new car. We went to a wedding reception held at a polo club. The cars were parked on the polo field. The kids had a tree house to play in that overlooked the polo field. My son decided to see how far the polo ball could fly out of the tree house window, forgetting that there were cars below them. He put a nice dent in the hood of a brand new car. The damage was close to $300. Our auto insurance wouldn't cover it, but our homeowner's policy did (less our deductible). It was the owner of the car who suggested we look into the homeowner's policy. He knew about it from his own son's growing-up years.

- The same goes for items that are stolen out of or damaged accidentally by your car. They are covered under the home-owner's policy.
- If you have an accident (such as tripping over the seat belt as you get out of the car) that incurs medical expenses, these would be covered by the medical portion of your car insurance.
- If you rent a car and it is stolen or wrecked, some automobile insurance policies cover you. Check with your agent before you waive the rental company's coverage.

ℒIFE INSURANCE

Life insurance is one of those necessary evils in life. It's something we'd probably rather not think about. It is there to provide for loved ones in order to protect their lifestyle after the bread-winner dies. Some people may not need much life insurance. Young people will most likely have no one to provide for, but may want a minimal policy to cover funeral expenses and outstanding debts. People without dependents or whose children are grown and independent, or those leaving no debts to their survivors, could do without life insurance.

I know of several families who carry no insurance. Most of these are barely able to provide for the family with what they bring home. This is a hard call to make, but I hope they are considering the financial devastation that may follow the husband or wife's death without insurance. Some expect Social Security to take care of their needs. This is not a good idea, since the future stability of that institution is in question at the moment, and the amount that Social Security pays is barely enough to pay the rent. Many families somehow come up with the money for cable TV, toys for the kids, or theater tickets but cannot seem to afford insurance. Most families can get a decent policy for less than $50 per month.

There are two main types of life insurance: term life and cash value. Following is a brief description along with some pros and cons of each type.

Term Life Insurance

A term policy provides the face value of the benefit and no more. Premiums are lower in the younger years and increase as you age. Consumer groups recommend this type of policy.

There are different types of term life insurance. Mortgage insurance is a type of term life insurance, called decreasing term life insurance. The premium remains the same, but its value shrinks over time as the mortgage balance shrinks.

Pros:

- Your premiums will be lower (up to 80 percent lower than cash value insurance) during your younger years for the same benefit amount as cash value insurance.
- You are free to invest the money you're not spending on the more costly cash value insurance where you can have better control and decision-making power; your investments will probably get a greater rate of return than the cash value insurance would deliver.
- You pay a lower commission fee (up to a 20 percent savings).

Cons:

- Your premiums will increase as you age.
- Coverage may terminate at the end of the policy's term. Some policies are not renewable. This could be a problem, since obtaining insurance at an older age can be more difficult and expensive.

Cash Value Life Insurance

These policies accrue interest over the life of the policy. They have a variety of names: annuity plans, endowment plans, variable life insurance, traditional whole life, single-premium whole life, interest-sensitive whole life, and universal life insurance.

They cost more than term policies because they provide both a life insurance coverage as well as an investment. This is the type of policy that most insurance agents recommend, however most consumer groups do not.

Pros:

- The premiums will remain stable as the insured person gets older.
- If the policy is not used by retirement age, it can be used as income.
- Some policies can be guaranteed for life.
- The IRS will not usually tax you on the earnings you are accruing.

Cons:

- Your premiums are higher in the early years for the same benefit amount as a term insurance premium.
- You cannot control the earnings on the investment amount.
- You may earn more elsewhere with your investment because the insurance company must pay a financial manager with a portion of your proceeds.
- Some types of cash-value policies do not pay the beneficiary the investment portion of their policy. In other words, if you took out a policy amount of $100,000, and you had accrued $15,000 in investment, when you die, the benefit amount paid to the beneficiary is only $100,000, not $115,000.

Where to Buy

After you have decided what type of life insurance to buy, the next question is who to buy it from. There are close to two thousand companies that sell life insurance, all wanting your business.

Some will provide better service, while others will provide better financial stability or a better return on your money.

To better understand your policy or your coverage needs, contact the National Insurance Consumer Organization, 121 Payne St., Alexandria, VA 22314, (800) 942-4242 or (703) 549-8050. They are a division of the Insurance Information Institute (800) 331-9146.

To get a rating on a company, call A.M. Best at (908) 439-2200. You are looking for an A or better rating.

To find out the financial strength of an insurance company, contact Weiss Research. They will prepare a verbal report for $15, a one-page brief for $25, or an extensive twenty-page report for $45. Or look on the Internet for Insurance News Network for a free peek at the company's financial strength (*www.insure.com*).

Many services will offer you quotes on life insurance. Some carry more companies in their database than others. Most of these services are free to you since the insurance companies pay for the service. But not all companies want to pay this fee, so not all are listed when you call for a quote. If there are some companies you are interested in, call them yourself.

Free Quote Services

company	phone number	Internet address	companies quoted
LifeRates	(800) 457-2837	none	200
MasterQuote	(800) 337-LIFE	*www.masterquote.com*	200
AccuQuote	(800) 442-9899	*www2.accuquote.com*	190
Quotesmith	(800) 431-1147	*www.quotesmith.com*	132
TermQuote	(800) 444-8376	*www.termquote.com*	10
SelectQuote	(800) 343-1985	*www.selectquote.com*	18
InsuranceQuote	(800) 972-1104	*www.iquote.com*	80

When you call for a quote, many companies require lots of information, so be prepared. Some information they may want includes your cholesterol count, blood pressure, weight, height, etc.

Ways to Save

For the best savings, sometimes up to 50 percent over outside agencies, take advantage of any group policies that you may be eligible for. Look for them in your workplace, clubs, spouse's clubs or service groups, universities, fraternities, unions, and military organizations. Many employers offer two times the employee's annual salary as a free benefit and then allow the purchase of subsequent coverage at a low fee. This will be your best deal.

To the insurance company we are a statistic: a group type, a risk category, and an age bracket. These are what will determine our costs for coverage. But not all companies consider the same statistic to be at the same level of risk. For example, one company may consider the area where you live as more risky than another company does. So shop around.

Try to lower your premiums before you shop. One way you can is to stop smoking. That alone can save you a bundle. Many insurers charge double to insure a smoker. Make sure that your weight falls into their desired category. It may pay to lose a few pounds.

Consider mail order insurance providers. Their premiums will be lower because they have no insurance agent's commission to pay. This can save you as much as 20 percent.

And the Winner Is . . .

The lowest rates available usually go to someone who falls into all of these categories:

- nonsmoker for the past four years
- normal blood pressure without medication
- no serious illnesses
- not overweight (according to the insurance charts)
- low cholesterol
- no deaths in the immediate family from heart disease before age sixty

Another way to save as much as 35 percent is to purchase a policy with your spouse. This type is called a first-to-die policy, and it pays just like it sounds. This is cheaper than two individual policies.

Insuring a child is not recommended, because life insurance is meant to provide for those left behind who depended on that person for income.

When buying a policy, ask for any future rate guarantees they can provide and whether the policy is renewable.

Avoid special travel insurance like that sold in airports. Travel is usually covered by general life insurance policies, making these special policies unnecessary.

How Much to Buy

The key to providing for your family is to assess their needs. How long do you want them to live as they are currently living? That could mean allowing for your spouse not to return to work for an extended period of time. Or perhaps the spouse does not currently work. Then you would want to provide for your current income for a period of time.

The period of time needs to be decided upon by the couple. How long do they want that current level of income? Some financial counselors recommend between five and ten years worth of expenses.

Other factors to take into consideration are any outstanding debts that would be left to the family, any business loans, taxes that would be due on the sale of a business, medical bills, estate taxes, moving costs if applicable, college tuition for the children, and mortgages.

To calculate the amount you will need, first remember that you will most likely not pay taxes on this income, so the annual amount needed is less than the annual salary being made now. Take the current annual salary and deduct any taxes being paid. Multiply this amount by the number of years you want to provide for. Then add in any extra expenses that may be needed in the future, as listed above. This will be the benefit amount that you should obtain a policy for.

Life Insurance Needs

Gross Annual Income   _____

Taxes Paid Annually   (_____)

Total Annual Need   (1)   _____

Future Special Expenses:
    mortgage balance   _____
    business debts   _____
    taxes (sale of business)   _____

college tuition		_____
funeral expenses		_____
medical bills		_____
estate taxes		_____
other		_____
Total Other Expenses	(2)	_____
Total Annual Need	(1+2)	_____
Number of Years Coverage	×	_____
Benefit Needed	=	_____
Assets Available	−	_____
cash/savings	−	_____
stocks	−	_____
401K	−	_____
Total Benefit Needed	=	_____

The Bottom Line

Once you have decided on what amount, what type, and from whom you will buy life insurance, remember that you are the consumer. If you feel uncomfortable about the policy you just signed, you have a few days to change your mind—risk-free. Some states allow as many as ten days for the free-trial period, while some allow only three days. Ask about this when you talk to the agent or sales company.

Coverage You Didn't Know You Had

Many of us are covered for life insurance through credit card companies and jobs. The amount of the policy may not be much, but it is worth investigating. Many credit cards automatically cover you for $5,000 of life insurance, and many employers cover their employees if they are killed while working (such as traveling on a business trip and the plane crashes). This is in addition to the policies you purchased through the same employer.

Other sources of income after a spouse dies are Social Security (burial fee and other possible benefits, (800) 772-1213) or veterans' benefits (check with the Veterans' Administration to see if you qualify: (800) 827-1000). If you are at least sixty years old and become widowed, you may collect on your husband. If you are a disabled widow, you can collect at age fifty. If you are divorced and your marriage lasted at least ten years, you may collect your ex's Social Security. Your children should collect Social Security if one parent dies—even if you are divorced.

MEDICAL INSURANCE

Nothing can wipe out your savings, current assets, and future plans faster than an uninsured medical situation. A long stay in a hospital can cost $50,000 or more. This will throw your plans for retirement, savings, and even home ownership into chaos. It's not worth the risk.

I know of a family who said they couldn't afford medical insurance, so they didn't buy any. They weren't poor and had money for other items some might consider nonessential. The mother of this large family had a freak accident and needed hundreds of thousands of dollars in care and surgeries. They asked others in their friendship circle and communities to bail them out because they hadn't planned ahead. Later we'll look at affordable plans for families in tight times like this one.

Another reason to carry medical insurance is that you will always be treated better if you have the insurance. Many doctors and hospitals won't provide care or will provide care with less quality and attention than with their paying patients.

Where

When you decide what the right type of insurance is for you and your family, start doing some comparative shopping. The most accessible and the cheapest place to get insurance is through your employer or your spouse's employer. If neither you nor your spouse have an employer policy available, other places to look are through any professional groups that you belong to, your college's alumni association, your automobile insurance carrier, trade organizations, the military service branch you served in, clubs, credit card companies, AARP, or any school you may be attending. Buying a policy as an individual will cost you 15–40 percent more than going in with a group. If you are not a member of a group or trade organization, consider joining one to get the group policy. If you are self-employed, membership in the National Association for Self-Employment ((800) 232-6273—*http://nase.org*) might offer a group discount. Remember that if you are self-employed, a large portion of your health insurance premiums is tax deductible.

If you are unhappy with the coverage available to you or you have some insurance coverage changes pending, check out other alternatives.

Other Options

Individual Policies

There are companies that cater to the individual instead of the group. These are worth looking into if you are self-employed or are not covered under any other group plan. Some even offer policies just for your kids. One company offers great coverage for a child for $35 per month. Examples of companies like this are Blue Cross Blue Shield, Mutual of Omaha, QualMed, Kaiser Permanente, etc.

Short-Term Policies

You can purchase short-term policies to cover you during brief periods of change. These can range from two to six months and work much like traditional insurance policies, covering major medical needs, with deductibles and co-payments. These usually do not cover preexisting conditions.

High Deductible Policies

There are high deductible policies that cost very little and will cover you in the event of a costly emergency. These will not cover routine medical needs but will cover anything over $2,500 or $5,000. The monthly rate on these varies across the country, but would run from $85–$150 per month for a family of four. This is better than the average independent comprehensive coverage policy cost of $600 per month for a family. Most major medical companies offer these. If this is the route you want to take, buy directly from the carrier. It could save you as much as 10 percent of the premium.

Hospital Indemnity Policies

High deductible policies are not to be confused with hospital indemnity policies. These offer $100–$200 per day in hospital room charges. If you have an emergency, your fees will run closer to $900–$1,000 per day. Get a comprehensive policy instead.

Sharing Groups

There are other options, many of which are not-for-profit organizations. There are groups of people forming their own sharing groups. These are for people who cannot afford regular insurance policies but who want to be covered in case of a major medical illness or accident. These policies usually do not cover regular doctor appointments but only major illness or injury. The groups usually require the member be a professing Christian, adhere to a lifestyle as defined in the Bible, and attend church regularly. The members of these groups share the costs of other members' medical needs after a deductible is paid. The cost per month for a family can be $60–$175, depending on the amount of deductible you choose.

Here are a few of these groups:

- Samaritan Ministries
  www.samaritanministries.org
  (888) 268-4377
- Medi-Share (division of the American Evangelistic Association)
  www.tccm.org
  (800) PSALM-23
- Christian Brotherhood
  www.cbnews.org
  (800) 910-4226

For those who are not eligible for group plans elsewhere and cannot afford an independent policy with full medical coverage on their own, this is a wise alternative. The woman in my earlier story who relied on the community to help her might have avoided the financial hardship by getting this type of policy.

Government Agencies

If none of these appeals to you or fits your needs, local government agencies such as the state Medicare office should also offer affordable insurance to anyone. You can find your local office by checking in the phone book or calling (800) 633-4227.

Switching Jobs

If you leave a job (other than being fired) you will most likely qualify for COBRA coverage (Consolidated Omnibus Budget Reconciliation Act). COBRA is a federal law that requires an employer to offer employees and their dependents the opportunity to purchase continuation of health care coverage in certain circumstances when company-paid health benefits end. This allows you to continue the coverage you had for up to eighteen months if the coverage cancellation was caused by layoff, resignation, leave of absence, or reduced work hours. If the loss of coverage was due to death of the employee, divorce, or a dependent child becoming ineligible, then the coverage can continue up to thirty-six months. The premiums will be higher than you were paying because of the loss of the employee discount, but it may be cheaper than your alternatives.

COBRA may be a good choice if you are changing jobs and have new insurance but you have either a waiting period or a pre-existing condition that won't be covered for a period of time.

We used COBRA once when my husband's employer went out of business. Beau was doing temporary work for a while until he could find something permanent. We had just had a baby and needed medical coverage. After checking into an independent policy through our insurance carrier and Blue Shield, we found COBRA cost us less.

Important Tips

COBRA will not be offered if the employer has fewer than twenty people.

Coverage in COBRA will cease if:

- You are late on a premium payment.
- You are eligible for COBRA due to a divorce and you remarry.

- You become eligible under another group insurance plan due to employment.
- The employer providing COBRA ends the group plan for all employees.

Converting to COBRA does not require waiting periods, qualifying for coverage, or exclusion of preexisting conditions.

Coverage sometimes covers less under COBRA. Ask before you sign up.

Remember, your costs will be higher, since you have lost the group discount.

Types of Coverage

When I shop for insurance, the first thing I consider is the type of care I want. Is it important to me to have a doctor whom I know and whom I can always see each time I need to? Will I get the best testing done for a problem I encounter? Can I go where I think I need to? The answers to these questions will direct you to the type of carrier you should choose.

Traditional 80/20

Traditional medical insurance pays for services. This type of plan usually has a deductible per person that must be paid out of your pocket before coverage begins, and then only 80 percent is covered. Make sure you understand what is covered.

Disadvantages: You pay the deductible out of your pocket, your portion of each visit is higher than in an HMO, and you have to deal with the billing paperwork.

Advantages: You can choose the doctor.

Managed Care

You pay a flat monthly fee, use the provider's medical doctors, and get most everything you will need.

Disadvantages: Because the insurance provider makes more money with less care provided to you, you may have to fight for the care you think you need.

Advantages: Because the provider wants less major medical bills, it will emphasize preventive care more than the 80/20 type.

HMO

Like managed care, but in an HMO (health maintenance organization) you get a broader choice of doctors, and your fee includes a small co-payment for each type of coverage.

Disadvantages: There are waiting periods for tests or specialists, since your primary physician must approve all care. You are also limited as to the doctors you can use, and emergency room visits must be limited to life-threatening status or you may be charged for them.

Advantages: More items are covered than through traditional coverage, there are no deductibles, preventive medicine is usually covered, the premiums are lower, and there is less paper work.

PPO

Like managed care; the preferred provider organization is a list of doctors who have agreed to provide service at a fixed fee. You can use other doctors and pay a higher co-payment.

What to Look for in Medical Coverage

- Inpatient hospital services
- Surgical services
- Ambulance coverage
- Doctor office visits
- Dependent coverage
- Newborn coverage
- Maternity care
- Cesarean coverage
- Annual exams/preventive care
- Prescriptions
- Laboratory work/tests
- X rays
- Physical therapy
- Home health care if needed
- Mental health coverage
- Drug and alcohol abuse treatment

Choosing an Insurance Carrier

Many people make a superficial decision about which medical insurance carrier to choose. Some decide because they prefer the ease of a co-payment rather than submitting an insurance form for reimbursement. Our decision for our care should go beyond convenience. We should look at the type of care we'll receive as well as the annual costs between carriers.

Some of the things to check for are:

Strength of the Company

Weiss Research will research the financial strength of most insurance organizations. A verbal report runs $15, with a one-page brief costing $25, and a detailed twenty-page report costing $45 ((800) 289-9222, *www.weissratings.com*).

To check on how dissatisfied past patients have been with denials for coverage, etc., ask the HMO for its disenrollment rate. It should be less than 15 percent.

Maximum Coverage per Lifetime

Preferably there is no maximum, since a long illness can run that limit out quickly. Seek out a company that has a $1 million per person lifetime cap.

Deductibles

Are they per person or per family? Per family is best if there are children. Pay as high a deductible as you can. You want to only pay for coverage of losses that you cannot afford. The higher the deductible, the lower the payments.

Duplicate Coverage

Make sure you are not paying for coverage twice: one policy for your spouse and one for yourself. Having a special policy for a disease plus comprehensive coverage is unnecessary (unless the comprehensive policy specifically excludes that disease). You can't be reimbursed twice for the same medical cost.

Exclusions

Some policies will not cover certain things. Check the fine print before signing. Typical exclusions are:

- Preexisting conditions. There is usually non-coverage and/or waiting periods for a preexisting condition. A preexisting condition can be defined as the existence of a symptom that a person received treatment for within a five-year period. This means a car accident with a back injury could render the back injury not covered, or long-term diabetes might not be covered. HMOs typically offer better coverage for preexisting conditions.
- Substance abuse
- Attempted suicide
- Mental illness
- Worker's compensation claims
- Cosmetic surgery
- Pregnancy
- Eyeglasses
- Dental work

Some people with preexisting conditions will never have to deal with exclusions, according to the Health Insurance Portability and Accountability Act of 1996. This act does not allow a new insurer to deny or delay coverage for a preexisting condition if you were with a group plan for eighteen months (or utilized COBRA for as long as you could) prior to signing on with them.

Specialists

If anyone in your family has a condition that requires ongoing care from a specialist (epilepsy, allergies, asthma, etc.), check if your insurance carrier will allow you to take her to a specialist and if the company has the type of specialist that you need on the plan.

Cancellation Policy

Check to see if your insurer can cancel your policy. How much warning is the insurer required to give you? For what reasons can they cancel your policy?

Renewability

This is usually a consumer right, but check to make sure. You don't want to lose coverage, especially if you become ill and cannot get coverage for your condition with a new company.

Other Considerations

Waiting period. Is there any waiting period before you are covered?

Durable medical equipment. This includes wheelchairs, respirators, and CPAP machines (for sleep apnea). They should pay 100 percent, but many are offering 50 percent. Go for the better deal.

Which hospitals are covered? Make sure they are ones with good records and not merely the cheapest ones around.

Amount of hospital coverage. Some carriers only cover a certain dollar amount for the hospital room. That may be insufficient, as rooms can cost up to $1,000 per day. Make sure your policy covers a percentage of your room costs.

Emergencies. When is an emergency room visit covered?

Comparison Shopping

When you are ready to purchase medical insurance, estimate what your medical needs will be over the next year. First, list what you needed last year. Then consider things such as the types of hospital services you may need, surgeries, prescriptions, ambulance, well baby care, maternity, physical therapy, out-of-town coverage, chronic illness coverage, and any annual cap on what you will spend. Then factor in the potential carrier's portion. Make sure to consider all types of carriers: HMO, PPO, indemnity (80/20). Below is our comparison of different types of carriers that we evaluated. By doing this sort of evaluation, we saved $300 per year.

Expenses per Year	Carrier		
	A	B	C
Premium (family of 4)	$500	$700	$1000
Deductible	200	0	0
Doctor's visits:			
2 kids annual exams	30*	0	0
5 unplanned visits	45*	25†	25†
Emergency (stitches, etc.)	75*	25‡	25‡
Chiropractor (average 6 per year)	60*	0	150‡
Medications (some plans won't cover certain drugs)	20	100	100
Annual Cost	$930	$1,150	$1,300

*20 percent is our portion
†$5 co-payment per visit
‡$25 co-payment per visit

Once you have selected a carrier, find out about their policy on visits to urgent-care facilities and emergency rooms. One type of service might be covered at a very different rate than the other. Also, some carriers restrict the coverage of certain types of visits to urgent-care facilities and emergency rooms and even might refuse to pay.

The Bottom Line

A few more things to remember when choosing insurance:

- Don't always assume that cheaper is better. Check out the reputation of the carrier.
- Don't underinsure you or your family. Living without medical insurance is much like playing roulette. The time will come when you will need it.
- Consider your need (or lack of need) for accidental death insurance. You are more likely to become disabled than to die from an accident—unless, of course, you are very reckless. Also, heart attacks are not considered accidents.

Pay premiums on time! A lapse of premium makes a lack of coverage. And before having a procedure or surgery, check with the insurance company to make sure you are covered and have the proper preapproval. You don't want to be hit with a surprise bill!

$\mathcal{D}$ISABILITY INSURANCE

The term *disabled* means that you are unable to perform your *usual work* for an extended period of time. If, after two years, you still have not returned to work, you qualify for Medicare. Many people think disability insurance is more important than life insurance. A thirty-year-old adult has a one-in-four chance of being disabled for up to a year. Can you and your family live on savings for a year? Disability insurance covers these things.

The benefit usually covers lost employment income. No policy pays for all lost income but will pay for part of it. This provides an incentive for you to return to work. These benefits are usually tax-free.

If you have many assets, insurers will be hesitant to provide you with disability insurance. They assume that you will not be motivated to return to work since you can live off your assets. Working at home is also a concern for insurers, as they cannot verify if you have returned to work or not.

To Save With Disability Insurance

- Increase the length of the waiting period before benefits begin. Increasing it to 90 or 180 days after loss of work can sometimes save as much as 25 percent.
- Reduce the percentage of benefits that you will receive once disabled. Make sure, however, that you get coverage for 60 percent of your income. Any less will be insufficient for your needs.
- Shorten the length of time you will be covered.

Exclusions

The following things will not be covered by disability insurance:

- Suicide attempts that leave you unable to work for physical or emotional reasons.
- Drug abuse that leaves you unable to work.
- Noncommercial plane crashes are not covered unless you were on the ground and not in the plane.
- Military acts or war.
- Normal pregnancy—since medical leave will usually cover this.

$\mathcal{V}$ISION

Many policies do not cover eye care, but we can't ignore our eyesight. If vision insurance is too costly for you, consider paying for an exam yourself. There are inexpensive alternatives to an ophthalmologist's exam, which can cost up to $100. An ophthalmologist is a complete doctor of the eye, treating both diseases of the eye as well as vision correction. Unless you have a serious eye problem, one alternative is to ask an optometrist to provide the exam and a prescription. Optometrists can screen and treat vision problems but cannot treat diseases of the eye. Their fees are usually one-fifth what an ophthalmologist charges. Make sure that the exam is thorough, including an exam of the inner eye (done with dilating drops).

Another option is to check with your local health department to find who in your area may provide free or very inexpensive exams. Also keep in mind that unless you are elderly or have a serious eye problem, an annual exam is not necessary. Every two or three years is sufficient. The health department also may have sources that provide inexpensive or free glasses.

Getting glasses can be expensive. Don't feel obligated to use the services of your eye doctor for filling the prescription. Shop around. Some of the discount chains that offer glasses give poor quality, while others have excellent reputations. Ask around, and call the Better Business Bureau for any complaints that may have been made.

For contact lenses, don't forget to look at mail order. This is an inexpensive and excellent alternative. Some companies to try are 1-800-CONTACTS, Factory Direct Lens (800-516-5367), and 1-800-LENS-EXPRESS.

$\mathcal{D}$OCTOR BILLS

When you do finally use the insurance carrier, find ways to reduce the doctor's bill. Sometimes doctors act as though it is our privilege to be seen by them, whereas we are actually hiring the doctor. And as with any work for hire, the fee needs to be discussed. Some doctors will write off your portion of the bill if you show financial need. Ask the carrier how you can reduce your part of the bill.

Here are some tips on how to reduce the doctor's bill:

- If you are on an 80/20 plan and think your portion of the bill is too high, find out what an HMO would pay. Ask the doctor if you can pay what the HMO patient would have paid.
- Use the carrier's preferred doctors and save 40 percent.
- Use the phone as often as possible instead of making an appointment. Many doctors will advise you and even prescribe medication over the phone. You can save the cost and the hassle of an office visit by "letting your fingers do the walking."
- See a general practitioner as often as possible rather than a specialist. They charge up to 40 percent less than specialists. Save the specialists for when it is necessary.
- Check out what your local county board of health has to offer. Many offer immunizations for children for free or for a minimal fee of $5. A visit to the doctor for the same service can run $75.
- Ask what the doctor charges. If you have a traditional 80/20 plan, this is essential. Not everyone charges the same rate. Rates can vary from $20 to $200 for an office visit.
- Avoid the emergency room. Use preventive care and common sense. Can it wait until morning when the office opens? Can you talk with the doctor over the phone and get the advice you need to get through the night? If this will work, you can save 50 percent of the doctor's fee plus the emergency room fee. (Many people who don't have insurance don't go to a doctor until their illness turns into a full-blown infection or pneumonia; then they go to emergency care. This is more costly than going to a doctor and paying cash.)
- Ask if the tests are necessary. What will they reveal? What alternatives are there to the tests? Some doctors profit from the

tests. For example, if they have their own X-ray equipment, they tend to order four times more X rays than those who use an outside service.

- Check around for a cheaper laboratory. I found a cheaper lab for blood sugar screening (half the price) by calling all the ones covered by my plan.
- Don't allow duplicate testing to be done. Sometimes if you switch doctors or get a second opinion, they want to redo the tests with their lab. There is no reason for this unless there is something really wrong with the quality of the first tests.
- Don't pay for the repeat of a test that the lab botched or lost.
- Get a second opinion. If it's for surgery or a course of treatment of which you question the necessity, the cost of another opinion will outweigh the cost of the wrong diagnosis.
- Read up on home treatments. Many office visits can be avoided for ailments for which the doctor can't do much to help you. Consider buying a medical guidebook. Check a few out from the library first to see which one you like best.

If you do get stuck with a fee that you didn't expect or cannot afford, try these time-honored approaches:

- Tell the doctor of your circumstances.
- Ask if there is a discount for paying your portion of the fee at the time of service.
- Will the doctor waive the co-payment?
- Will the doctor take small monthly payments?
- If you are going through a hard time financially, ask the doctor for a reduced fee. Many would rather you get the care you need and get paid less than have you go without care.

$\mathcal{H}$OSPITAL BILLS

Hospital bills account for a majority of the amount spent in the U.S. for health care. The best way to avoid the high cost of hospitalization is to make sure that you need to be there. Many surgeries are not necessary or are subjective. Forty percent of hospital admittance is not necessary. Get a second opinion before committing to anything.

Often admittance is to comfort and provide care that the

patient may not get at home. Sometimes that is needed. But maybe there needs to be some reconsideration when the doc says, "Let's check you in."

Doctors handle medical situations in many ways. And it is important that we speak up if we think there may be a better way. One example of how different doctors do things is when my husband had kidney stones. In California, each attack was treated on an outpatient basis. He was given pain-killers in the emergency room and then sent home until the stone passed or he could get an appointment for the "stone crusher" (lithotripsy). We were often shuttling back and forth to the emergency room for better pain-killers when the stone bothered him.

In Colorado, his attack warranted a three-day hospital stay. They did nothing for him other than maintain the level of pain-killer and make him comfortable. It was better for his comfort but more costly. In order to meet aggressive health care cuts, California insurance companies keep people out of the hospital as much as possible. Births get you home in twenty-four hours, and kidney stones and most surgeries are done on an outpatient basis.

Questions You Should Ask Before Agreeing to Hospital Admittance

- Can this be done as an outpatient?
- Will my surgery be done as "open surgery" or as a minimally invasive surgery? The latter can usually be done as outpatient and requires less healing time.
- Should I be treated somewhere else (home heath care, nursing home)?
- Is surgery necessary? Are there other ways to treat this?

Choosing a Hospital

Most of us can choose the hospital we want to go to. Unless our doctor is limited to one hospital or our insurance carrier limits us, we can make a choice. When choosing, we need to remember that not all hospitals offer the same fees or quality of care. Both should be investigated.

Fees

The fees that hospitals charge vary greatly. Beau had two hospitalizations in the same town but with drastically different price tags. His first stay was at a hospital in a lower-income part of town. He stayed for three days in intensive care. That bill was $8,000. He had another stay in a hospital in a higher-income part of town for four hours in outpatient surgery, which had a price tag of $16,000. It really pays to check around for fees. Don't be afraid to call and ask.

Price shouldn't be the only consideration for something as important as hospital care. Take into consideration the quality of care a facility provides. Teaching hospitals tend to be more expensive, and insurance companies often

---

Save 50 Percent on Hospital Bills

Try an urgent care center before a hospital's emergency room if you can. The urgent care centers charge 50 percent less than hospital admissions.

---

do not cover them. The city-run or -sponsored hospitals tend to be cheaper but provide poorer service. To find these, ask where the police take accident victims or the uninsured.

Most people assume that a hospital bill is a fixed fee. In many cases it is, but this is not always true. Many hospitals are very understanding and will accept whatever the insurance company will cover combined with whatever you are able to pay. To make this arrangement, you will need to plead your case and possibly offer documentation to support it. Many large bills can be negotiated, especially if the hospital is in a lower-income area. These hospitals have many customers who simply can't pay for their visit, so the hospital has to write off the cost. If a customer can pay but needs to make small payments, the administrators usually cooperate to get their money.

After my husband's three days in intensive care, twelve various bills arrived for our portion after insurance. We could only afford to pay each $10 per month. All of them were willing to accept these terms, and none ever charged interest. For the trip to the hospital that cost $16,000, the hospital did not want to accept payments for our portion of the bill. Instead, it offered us a 20 percent discount if we paid by the end of that month. That added up to a large savings and was worth doing what we had to in order to pay the bill by the end of the month.

Don't be afraid to contest the amount that the insurance company decides to cover. There are human beings with tender hearts working at these companies. I have had medications and procedures covered that normally would not be, just because I wrote a sincere and explanatory letter regarding the situation. Send supporting documents, such as a doctor's letter, if you can.

Quality

Finding the right hospital can be just as important as getting the right price. To find a good hospital in your area, ask your doctor's opinion.

You can also ask the hospital for its track record. What is the average length of stay and the mortality rate for each type of illness and surgery? The hospital keeps these statistics.

Check out the Consumer's Guide to Hospitals published by the Center for the Study of Services (800-231-7283). It provides death rates, background information, and percentage of doctors that are board certified in many hospitals. It will tell you each hospital's death rate for each type of procedure you may need. Ask your librarian for help finding this.

Check out the JCAHO (Joint Commission on Accreditation of Heath Care Organizations) at *www.jcaho.org*. They award accreditation to hospitals by evaluating guidelines for quality of care and services, procedures in intensive care, record-keeping, and safety of equipment. Their questions hotline is (630) 792-5000.

Cutting Costs When Hospitalized

If you need to be in a hospital, you have selected a hospital that you are comfortable with, and you know what to expect of the fees, there is one more step you can take. You can reduce some of the expenses while you are there. Try these out to save a few dollars:

- Check in and out according to the hospital's schedule. If you stay after the hospital's check-out time, you will be charged an extra day, much like a hotel. The same goes for check-in time.

Find out when the check-in time is, and don't come before that. Billing is usually done by calendar days and not twenty-four-hour periods.

- Avoid checking in on Fridays. Most hospital services are not available over the weekend, so you are paying for a few unnecessary days.
- Make sure your testing isn't what is holding you up. If you need a certain test in order to be discharged and the lab is running late, you may be held another day for that test. Demand that it be done in a timely manner, or ask that the test be done as an outpatient the next day.
- Bring your own linens (pillows, nightgown if allowed, slippers). These can run up to $300 per day! To save on these, you must inform the billing office of the hospital before you check in.
- Bring your own toiletries (shampoo, tissue, toothbrush, toothpaste, razors, etc.). A tissue box will run $4, and some razors have been charged at $14.
- If you are on daily medication prior to admittance, bring your own meds so the hospital can't charge you a big markup for filling your needs there.
- If you are waiting for a specialist to see you or for a consultation between your regular doctor and another doctor, don't let that delay keep you in. Call the consulting doctor's office if you need to speed things up.
- Ask questions: Why am I being discharged tomorrow and not today?
- Ask if preadmittance tests are necessary. Some are routine and have nothing to do with your condition. If you need them, can they be done before going to the hospital? They are cheaper if you are not a patient of the hospital.
- Check in the day of surgery and not the night before so another day's fee is saved.
- Check out as soon as possible. Ten percent of patients become ill at the hospital because so many infections can be picked up there.
- Review the bill carefully when it arrives. Nearly all hospital bills contain errors. Many of the errors are input mistakes, such as charging $110 for a pill instead of $1.10. Ask for the

bill to be itemized if it doesn't arrive that way. Review each charge and make sure you had that service done or item provided.

MEDICATIONS

By using generic versions of prescription and over-the-counter drugs you can save 30–80 percent over the cost of name-brand drugs. I have seen a drop from $100 to $20 for one prescription just by switching to the generic version of the drug. Even many over-the-counter drugs can have a large variance between a name brand and a generic version. In addition to using generic as often as possible, shop around. Many stores and warehouse clubs have varying rates for store-brand versions of drugs.

I have heard of people who won't buy generics and insist on using only name brands. They feel that the generic version is not as good. But the law requires that the generic version have the same active ingredients as the original name brand.

Others feel that the inventor of a medication needs to be encouraged to continue inventing new products. These consumers feel that if we only buy the generic version, the inventors cannot afford to continue their good work. We must remember that no one stole the formula for the generic version. Most generic drug formulas only come on the market after the original patent has expired. The original manufacturer holds this patent for many years (usually ten years) and makes a great deal of profit from the formula before it is made public. Much of the original research was done independently and then sold to a major manufacturer. Many of the big-name pharmaceutical companies didn't invent the drugs. That manufacturer also sells much of its original product to the generic companies to be resold as a generic brand.

Don't overlook mail order pharmacies such as Medi-Mail (800-331-1458). These are great for medications that you use regularly. They can give you a good discount, up to 60 percent off name-brand prescriptions. If you are a member of AARP (American Association of Retired Persons), it has arranged good pricing as well. Contact its pharmacy for details at (800) 456-2277.

For colds, I don't buy the all-in-one remedies that are advertised heavily. You take stuff that you don't need and pay for the convenience of having them combined. A bottle of decongestant with acetaminophen added will cost 20–30 percent more than if you buy them separately. Instead, know the ingredients and buy those generically. Keep several separate bottles in the cabinet— one for each type of medication. I keep a piece of paper taped to the inside of the medicine cabinet that tells me what each ingredient is meant to help. When I have a particular symptom, I take only that drug. Some people like the hot flu medication drink that is packaged for your convenience. Just take what you need (fever reducer, decongestant, etc.) and have a hot cup of herb tea or hot water with lemon juice and honey. The same effect will be achieved and will cost you less. Below is the list that is taped to my cabinet, in the hope it will help you.

Generic Names and Purposes for Cold Medications

dextromethorphan	for dry cough/cough suppressant
guaifenesin	for gooey cough/expectorant
pseudoephedrine	decongestant
ephedrine	decongestant
chlorpheniramine	antihistamine
diphenhydramine	antihistamine

It's important to know what you need. You can complicate your problems by using the wrong drug. For example, if you have a gooey cough, using a cough suppressant isn't a good idea. Ask your doctor or pharmacist before you self-medicate to be sure you're choosing the right medicine.

Another thing to keep in mind with any medication that you buy is to compare the unit price (the cost per milliliter or milligram). Sometimes it's cheaper to take two capsules of a smaller dose than to take one of a larger dose. This is particularly true of aspirins and other pain-killers. Again, you are paying for the convenience of having someone combine pills for you.

Other Ways to Save

- Are you popping pills all the time? Look into the cause of the trouble. Is it poor nutrition, an imbalanced diet, possibly not drinking enough water each day, or something more serious that requires a doctor's attention?

- Look into an alternative way of treating the problem. There is nutrition, chiropractic, acupuncture, exercise, support groups, etc. Do some research from all angles before relying on drugs. Medical doctors often won't encourage you to pursue these avenues because they are not trained or experienced in them.
- Consult a medical guide for treating yourself for common ailments.
- Sometimes saving a few dollars by avoiding a prescription is not as wise as taking the drug. I know people who try to cure strep throat naturally, for example. I think that's great if it works. But some people keep on getting it back. Strep throat is nothing to mess with, since it can develop into rheumatic fever if not treated. A course of penicillin is less harmful to your body than heart damage.
- Take advantage of senior citizen discounts. You qualify at the age of fifty-five.
- Shop at discount drugstores. This can save up to 40 percent.
- When buying over-the-counter drugs, buy the largest container size that you will consume over a six-month period. This will often save you 35 percent over the cost of several smaller containers.

Tips for Kids

Since chewable medicine is more costly than tablets, try these savings tips:

- Crush an adult tablet of the drug (make sure it's cut to the child's dose first) and mix with honey or jam.
- Getting kids to swallow a pill is helpful. Have them practice by swallowing M&Ms or Tic Tacs. Mistakes aren't nasty tasting.

Free Drugs

The pharmaceutical companies give many doctors free drugs as samples. They are meant to be given to patients.

For those who cannot afford their prescriptions, the Pharmaceutical Manufacturers' Association offers free medications. Eligibility requirements vary. Some drug manufacturers have strict financial hardship requirements, while others leave it up to the doctor's discretion. Whichever is used, a doctor must certify the patient's medical need for the drug and apply for you to the PMA. If your doctor is unfamiliar with this program, give him or her the PMA phone number (800-PMA-INFO).

Don't Save Money This Way

Don't try to save by not taking all of the doses that were prescribed in hopes of using them later. You may end up with a secondary problem that will cost more than the bottle of pills. For example, by not completing a course of antibiotics, you run the risk of building immunity to that antibiotic and having complications the next time you are sick. Even if you feel better, you need to finish the bottle.

Don't take over-the-counter drugs if your symptoms persist. See a doctor and stop the problem before it gets really serious and costly.

Check the expiration date on anything you take. Throw out expired medications. Some medications get stronger with age, while others weaken. Most poison control centers recommend flushing the drugs down the toilet to prevent children from finding the drugs in the trash and taking them. Environmental advocates fear flushed medications can affect water quality and aquatic life and recommend taking the expired drugs to your local hazardous waste site for incineration. Most pharmacies will not dispose of it for you, but it never hurts to ask.

DENTAL EXPENSES

Many people avoid going to the dentist. Not just because it's an uncomfortable encounter but because they are not covered by a health plan that includes a dental plan. Since they have to pay for all visits out of their own pockets, they tend to avoid preventive care and wait until it's too late or too costly to save a tooth.

Many employers can't afford dental insurance, thus leaving people on their own.

There are several dental plans available to the average person.

Some are under $100 per year and work like an HMO with you choosing from their selected dentists. These plans usually pay 100 percent of preventive care (cleanings, checkups, and basic fillings). Some national department store chains offer these plans (Sears, for example). Plans are also available through Medicaid and Medicare.

Whether you can afford dental insurance or not, here are some ways to make the most of your dental budget:

Prevention

As much as I hate to admit it, the dentists are right. Prevention is the best way. By brushing after meals, flossing, and getting regular cleanings, we prevent plaque from eating away the enamel and causing expensive cavities or root canal problems. I know this because I did not practice good dental care until a few years ago. And now I am paying for it. I don't mean that I was not brushing and flossing. I was doing both but either at the wrong times or not frequently enough. Most of us eat between meals without brushing. And many of us do not floss every night. When I learned that 35 percent of all gum disease and tooth loss is a result of plaque that destroys tooth enamel, I took notice. A root canal can cost $250 per tooth. You can buy a lot of dental floss and brushes for that. You can also save yourself some gum and enamel damage by using the right kind of brush and by brushing correctly. Listen to your dentist as he shows you the correct way.

Toothpaste is worth investigating. You don't need the big-name brands to have healthier teeth. You can also use less paste than the television commercials suggest. That will save a few cents with each brushing. When I was growing up overseas, we could not get toothpaste. We could order tooth powder, but when we ran out, we used the healthy standby—baking soda and salt. You can mix it with cinnamon, mint extract, or a flavored fluoride liquid to enhance the flavor. This is healthy for the teeth and gums and very cheap.

The whole idea of brushing is to keep the foods (particularly sugar) off of the teeth so plaque is discouraged from growing. So don't snack right after brushing. When you brush in the morning, do it after breakfast. The same principle applies to our kids. Don't let them snack or drink juice or milk all day. The constant food and sugars in the liquids are feeding the plaque. After they eat, brush their teeth. Have them snack on nonsugar items such as vegetables and water. Make sure they go to bed with clean teeth and no bottles or cups of juice or milk. The constant bath of juice (or milk) on their teeth eats away at the enamel. All of this may sound excessive, but it saves teeth and money.

Cleaning

The best preventive care is to have a professional cleaning twice a year. Plan for this in the budget. It is much cheaper than a root canal or extraction—with possible braces later due to a drifting bite from the missing tooth.

To save on professional cleanings, try a local dental school or community college. They charge as much as 75 percent less than a private dentist. Many county health departments also have dental facilities.

Dental and Orthodontic Work

To receive dental or orthodontic care at a lower cost, check into local universities and dental schools. Some have a dental program and offer low-cost appointments by students in training. Certified dentists always supervise these students. Even universities that do not offer dental schools can offer low-cost appointments by students who are mentoring under a certified dentist. The cost of an average visit is 50 percent less than a similar visit to a dentist in private practice. If you cannot afford much, check with your local county health department for low-cost dental services.

Other Ways to Save

Having X rays done annually is not necessary, says the American Dental Association. Unless there is a suspected problem, X rays for the entire mouth are needed only every three years.

Consider sealants for molars. They cost $20–$50 per tooth, but they protect against cavities for up to ten years. Fillings cost more than this and usually have to be replaced after a number of years.

Brushing the correct way with a good toothbrush is as effective as an electric or ultrasonic toothbrush and costs less.

Don't wait until something hurts to have it fixed. Most problems don't hurt until it's too late and may require expensive solutions.

Don't Save Money This Way

If you need special work done, such as a root canal, get a referral to a specialist (in this case, an endodontist). Paying the higher fee for a specialist to do it is well worth it because you avoid the risk of it not being done right. Someone who doesn't do the work correctly can cause cracked teeth or years of struggle with nerve damage and pain.

RESOURCES

Inlander, Charles B. *150 Ways to Be a Savvy Medical Consumer*. People's Medical Society, 1992.

Inlander, Charles B., and Karla Morales. *Getting the Most for Your Medical Dollar*. DIANE Publishing Company, 1997.

Kennedy, David. *How to Save Your Teeth: Toxic-Free Preventive Dentistry*, Health Action Press, 1996.

Nader, Ralph, and Wesley J. Smith. *Winning the Insurance Game*. Broadway Books, 1993.

Ulene, Art. *How to Cut Your Medical Bills*. Ulysses Press, 1994.

CHAPTER TWELVE

Help Around the House: Electrical Appliances

I think housework is the reason most women go to the office.

—Heloise, 1963

$ $ $

*G*otcha! You probably thought I was going to tell you how to get free maid service or something along those lines. After all, the Proverbs 31 woman of the Bible had handmaidens. Many people believe that is the only reason she could do all she did. Maybe, but maybe you have the same help too.

Some of us have a romantic notion of the olden days, where our ancestors had leisurely teas and strolled to the neighbors for a visit in the parlor. Some families lived in this manner, but most did not. Even those who had these luxuries of time did it with help. Someone else did the washing, cooking, cleaning, milking the cow, churning the butter, and making the clothes. These were the handmaidens of that day.

Servants seem like such a luxury to us. But back then it was quite common. Household budgets included wages for the help, just as our budgets include a washer, dryer, and refrigerator. At the turn of the last century, many families replaced their help with new inventions. Reasons varied for their replacement. With the post–Civil War exodus of workers to factories, electricity was brought into most neighborhoods, and servants were occasionally unreliable.

At first only the rich could afford these bulky machines. As they improved and more models were produced, the prices came down. Servants were replaced with "electrical handmaidens."

Even though our current help is electric in nature, it is just as valuable to us. It gives us the freedom to do other things with our life, just as servants gave our ancestors that freedom. Let's not forget how much work they had to do—with or without hired help—or we would have if we lived without our modern appliances:

- We don't chop the wood and then stoke the fire to make breakfast.

   We flick a switch on the stove.
- We don't milk the cow and churn the butter.

   We drop in at the local market.
- We don't drag the carpet outside and beat it.

   We vacuum it.
- We don't draw water from a pump, well, or river.

   We turn on a faucet.
- We don't sew all of our clothes (including underwear).

   We shop at Target.
- We don't draw ten gallons of water from a pump, drag it to the backyard tub, build a fire, boil the clothes, hang them, and then re-dye the faded ones.

   We use a washer and dryer.
- We don't dry, cure, and store foods for the winter.

   We shop at the local grocery store.
- We don't clean chamber pots every morning.

   We flush.
- We don't spend one-fifth of our waking hours washing the dishes.

   We have a dishwasher.

Now that we understand the origin and value of our electrical appliances, let's see how we can afford to buy them.

BUYING ELECTRICAL APPLIANCES

Buying appliances can be overwhelming. The salespeople think you should buy a particular model, your family wants another one, and you think a third type is ideal. Whom do you listen to? This chapter is not a consumer guide on which model to buy of which electrical appliance. There are plenty of consumer guides available. Rather, it is my hope to provide steps to go through before making your decision.

These steps can be applied to almost any item you are purchasing. Basically, three decisions need to be made.

1. Know What You Want

List all of the features that are essential to you. If you merely shop based on what looks nice or seems good, you will regret your decision later. Before you set out for the store, ask yourself if the new fridge needs spill-proof shelves, auto-defrost, or an icemaker. Does the washing machine need multispeed settings or is the simple version satisfactory? Does your camera need to be digital or is it okay to have 35mm and film?

If you are unfamiliar with the product you are buying because you have never used one regularly, ask people who have used it. A good example of this is a cell phone. More and more people are buying them, but many have never owned or used one before. Talk to people who have had them for a while. What do they wish they had or didn't have? What features did they later find were essential or perhaps unnecessary? What aspects of the service contract did they overlook? Learn from their experience.

Measure the space an appliance will take before you buy. Sometimes it doesn't fit after being delivered. Also check to be sure its features are compatible to the place it will occupy. You don't want to find out that there is room for the clothes dryer but not its vent hose, or that the new television may fit in the cabinet but its speakers on the sides will be blocked by wood.

2. Research the Choices

Once you know what features you want, check around for who makes the best model.

• List all of the companies that make the appliance you want to buy.

- Check consumer magazines at the library for reliability ratings on each manufacturer and model.
- Create a spreadsheet or grid of this information so it is easy to see which rates best.

Example of a Grid for Comparison Shopping

Manufacturer:	A	B	C
Model 1:			
safety	pass	fail	good
service	fail	pass	pass
overall	pass	pass	good
Model 2:			
safety	fail	pass	good
service	pass	pass	pass
overall	good	fail	fail
Model 3:			
safety	pass	good	fail
service	pass	pass	pass
overall	good	pass	pass

3. Do You Need New or Will Used Do?

Many thrifty folks buy used electrical appliances because they are more affordable. I can relate. When we moved to Colorado, all of our major appliances stayed with the house in California as a package deal. That meant we had to buy a washer, dryer, and refrigerator. We first looked at used appliances because of the sheer enormity of the cost. But after taking a closer look, we began to wonder if we needed to save up and go for new stuff.

Part of the problem we encountered was that often the used stuff was very old and the company selling it was questionable as to reputation and reliability to fix it if it broke down. When we looked in the paper for individuals selling appliances, their prices weren't too much less than new—maybe $75 less. But an individual cannot offer a warranty that the item will work once you get it home. So we felt like we were gambling with the purchase of a used model. And for a bit more we could get a new one with a warranty.

The other thing we became aware of was the cost of running the appliance. The new models are so energy efficient that overall they cost less to own. Appliances as "young" as five years old can use up to three times more energy than the newer ones. We checked the energy consumption of both used and new models and factored that in with the purchase price. We came out way ahead with new appliances.

Not everyone would agree with my decision, and many can get a more dramatic deal on a used model. Others may not be able to wait while they save the extra money needed to get a new one instead of a used one. If you fall into any of these categories, here are some tips to keep in mind when you are shopping for a used electrical appliance:

If Buying Used . . .

Make sure that the model you are getting has a good reliability rating. You need this extra leg up since it is used. Check at the library for information on older models, their service records, and general overall satisfaction ratings given by consumers. Some publications that carry this information are *Consumer Digest* and *Consumer Reports*.

If you are buying the item from a store, call your local Better Business Bureau and get the scoop on the store. Has it had complaints against the store's work and products? If so, skip buying from that store no matter how good the deal.

If the store checks out, make sure the unit has a warranty.

If you are buying from an individual, ask if he would be willing to take the unit back if it does not work within one week of delivery. Many appliances act up once unplugged and moved.

Make sure to allow for delivery of the item. Unless you have a truck or a friend who has one and is willing to help you, you may have to add $50 or more to the purchase in order to get the item home.

Check the energy rating. If it rates poorly in comparison to new models, the used one may actually cost you more over a few years than a new model would. If this is the case, it would be cheaper to save up and buy a new one.

If Buying New . . .

Sometimes used models aren't the best buy. Watching sales on new items can sometimes be a more frugal decision.

Look (and ask) for appliances that are blemished or have superficial defects. When we decided to buy new models, the cash was very tight. We watched sales and saved our pennies for months and found the best price we could. We went ready to buy a plain refrigerator that was advertised. When we got to the store we learned that there were some models on sale that had cosmetic defects, such as paint scratches. These were marked off an additional $150. We were able to get a new model for not much more than a used one would have been, and the blemishes were hard to find!

Know what a good sale price is. Small appliances such as microwaves have a markup of 30 percent. So a good sale should be 30 percent off retail. Major home appliances such as refrigerators and dryers have a markup of 15 percent.

Shop around for the models that came out on top in your research. One tip to get better pricing is to get a copy of the Sunday newspaper from a major city in the U.S. (you can get these at libraries and bookstores). Look for the home appliance flyers and see if they have better prices on the same make and model as your local flyers offer. If it is the same model and manufacturer, you can ask your local retailer to match that lower price. Good cities from which to check the Sunday paper are New York City (*New York Times*), Los Angeles (*LA Times*), and Chicago (*Chicago Tribune*).

Call the manufacturer and get the model numbers for last year's discontinued models. Ask for these at the department store to see if any are left (at a good discount price), or use this model number at the mail-order outlets (see the following list).

Consider some of the mail-order outlets. They offer goods at good discounts as well as full warranties that will be honored by most local repair centers. To use the mail-order outlets, you need to know the exact manufacturer name, model number, and description. Here are a few that carry appliances:

- 4Cost (appliances & electronics)
  (877) 654COST
  www.4cost.com
- EBA Wholesale (major appliances of over 50 name brands)
  (888) 728-3266
  http://eba.homeappliances.com
- Bernie's Discount Center (all types of electronics and appliances)
  821 Sixth Ave
  New York, NY 10001
  (212) 564-8582

RESOURCES

Cohen, Daniel. *The Last Hundred Years: Household Technology.* M. Evans & Co., 1982.

Gramm, Barbara Fairchild. *And You Think You've Got It Bad.* Independent Publishing, 1994.

Kleinert, Eric. *Troubleshooting and Repairing Major Appliances.* McGraw-Hill, 1995.

Rains, Darell L. *Major Home Appliances: A Commonsense Repair Manual.* Tab Books, 1987.

Schultz, Mort. *Fix It Yourself for Less.* Consumer Reports Books, 1992.

Wood, Robert W. *All Thumbs Guide to Repairing Major Home Appliances.* Tab Books, 1992.

CHAPTER THIRTEEN

Car Buying

A purpose without a plan is pitiful.
—Ronald and Barbara Sennert,
How to Save $9000 on Your Next Car or Van

$\mathcal{U}$nlike Europe—much of which has excellent mass transport systems—most of North America does not have even adequate public transportation. This is partly because of sheer size and partly because the vast majority of the population centers of this area of the world, unlike Europe, developed after the invention of the automobile. Unless you live in an urban or suburban area close to work, schools, shopping, and church, you will find a car indispensable.

But do you need a *second* car? The two-car family may be an American tradition, but many families can get along just fine with only one car. Since a car is the third largest expense a family incurs after housing and insurance, families on a tight budget would be wise to consider very carefully whether they really need two cars.

Many issues are involved in buying, keeping, and maintaining a car. Some of these include: Should it be a new or used car? Is it smarter to pay cash or finance it? Can I afford the higher insurance on this car? Do I want a foreign or domestic car? Should I sell my present car or trade it in? How do I know which cars are most reliable? Cheapest to operate and maintain? Safest?

One interesting thing about cars that is seldom thought about is that each country builds them along certain lines and with particular values in mind. For example, German cars are noted for their overall performance (Porsche, BMW). Italian cars have a certain spirit (Ferrari, Lamborghini). The Swedes are known for building the safest cars (Volvo, Saab). The French make exotic cars (Citroen). The British make racy cars (Jaguar, Aston Martin). Japanese cars are known for value and reliability (Nissan, Toyota, Honda). Korean cars are inexpensive (Hyundai, Kia). And American cars are practical (Chevrolet, Ford). Since a car is in some ways an extension of your personality, you might want to think about which aspects of a car are most important to you.

VALUE IN CARS

As in most material things, value in cars is subjective. What a college kid on a limited income regards as value will likely be a lot different from that of a middle-class mom of five. The college kid is looking for basic transportation; the mom of five needs lots of space and quite a bit of practicality. People who spend a good deal of time in their cars, such as traveling salesmen, will rate comfort and reliability as important values.

Another thing to consider when trying to determine any particular car's value is to think of value in terms of the total life of the car. If you plan to keep your car for a long time—say eight to ten years, or 150,000 miles or more—you will probably want a car that not only has an excellent reputation for durability but also is noted for low-cost maintenance. Fuel consumption should also be taken into consideration. If you are planning on having a car for a shorter time, resale value might be a major factor for you. Some cars retain their value much better than others, and that could mean you'll get more money at trade-in time and end up paying a lower price for your next car.

THESE ARE THE GOOD OLD DAYS

Fortunately for today's shopper looking to buy a car, these *are* the good old days. Cars today are more powerful, cheaper to run, more comfortable, safer, and more fun to drive. For example, it used to be that only the most expensive sports cars could deliver the performance that a number of today's sedans deliver routinely—and without being gas hogs. Seats are more comfortable, driving positions more natural, visibility better. Today's cars brake better, corner better, accelerate better, last longer, have better paint and finishes, and often are less costly to repair.

A good deal of this is probably a result of the excellence foreign manufacturers have brought to the North American car market. After all, in the U.S., for more than a decade, it usually has been the foreign car that has been the best selling car. This has spurred American car makers to put a better product on the market, and the competition with foreign companies has had the effect of raising the bar for the entire industry.

*B*UYING A NEW CAR

Unless you're one of the few people who loves to haggle, buying a car will probably cause you some anxiety. Even if you don't mind a little wheeling and dealing, you're probably still going to come out the loser when you go up against car dealers. They are experts at it and you're not. Haggling is what they do for a living—and that's not what most of us spend our days doing. They know every trick of the trade—not all of them completely above board—and they're perfectly prepared to use them on you, the unsuspecting victim.

One of the ways you can even the playing field is to go in prepared. For example, there are resources that will tell you the dealer invoice of any car you may want to buy. (For a list of these, see the resources at the end of this chapter.) Most car dealers will settle for somewhere around $500 over invoice, which is often thousands of dollars less than the sticker price. Edmunds Consumer Information on car buying recommends fair prices on cars (*www.edmunds.com*).

You also can be thoroughly knowledgeable about financing. Know your interest rates and what you can get elsewhere before discussing financing with the dealer. You can probably get a better deal elsewhere. Car dealers often make their biggest profits from financing and warranties. In fact, most car dealerships have a special department called finance and insurance (F&I). Their job is to get you to buy their products, which are often marked up 300 percent or more, or in the case of financing are several points above market value. Know your coverage under your current insurance policy before going into their insurance carrier's office.

Often car dealers offer what looks like a great deal but it covers nothing important. Some of their offerings include hundreds of dollars for rust proofing, which all cars already have; fabric protection, which is simply about $10 worth of Scotchgard for which you pay a couple hundred dollars; pinstriping, costing $300 or $400 and worth about one-third of that; gold trim, which isn't gold at all but anodized aluminum; extended warranties that cover things already covered by the factory warranty. One car dealership had a neat scam going. They had a built-in additional warranty as part of their invoice. When they asked buyers if they wanted the extra warranty and they declined, it was left in the invoice. If buyers accepted it, they were charged double.

Another trick car dealers often use is to try to get buyers' minds off the price of the car and on to what their monthly payment will be. If they can get customers to say what they want to pay per month, they can play around with financing figures, giving the buyer low payments but still ensuring that they make a large profit in the end.

Before making a final decision on any car, it is important to test-drive it. There are many things to check out in your test drive, so it is best if you can get the dealer to let you have the car for an extended period of time. After all, you are spending a lot of hard-earned money to buy a new car, and you will be spending a good deal of time in it. You should have the opportunity to thoroughly try it out.

You will want to check out many things on your test drive. In addition to the normal items such as handling, braking, and acceleration, feel your reactions to the environment of the car: Is the seat comfortable? Does it have enough support? Are all the controls logically placed and easily reachable? Would you feel good spending more than a few hours in the car? How well do the heater and air-conditioner work? Are road and wind noise levels acceptable? What about the driving position? Are you too high or too low? Does it have a good sound system? Is there adequate interior lighting? These are just a few things to think about.

You might also consider test-driving a couple of other cars in the same class, even if you're not seriously considering them, just to see how well the car you're interested in stacks up against them. You may surprise yourself by finding out that the hot little number you had your heart set on really doesn't hold up that well to the competition.

Bargains

Sometimes, especially if you're willing to delay gratification and perhaps settle for a car that is not your first choice, you can save thousands of dollars on a new car purchase. One way to save money is to go to a dealer at the end of a model year. Many times dealers are looking to clear out last year's models, and you can get spectacular savings—sometimes as much as $5,000 or more.

These good deals usually occur in the fall when the new models have arrived and the dealers need to clear out the old inventory. We got our minivan this way. We had saved enough for a used van and went to see one that a dealer was selling. The dealership next door had an incredibly low sale price for a brand-new minivan advertised on their window. We dropped by to see how we could get this price. After finding out that the price was after rebates and student discounts (which we didn't qualify for) we were going to leave. The salesperson asked us what we could afford, and we told him the total we had, plus our old car as a trade-in. This amounted to $5,000 less than the sticker price of the plainest model that they sold. We left knowing that we could never afford a new car. The dealer called us for three days, lowering the price each time. He couldn't lower the price of the car any more, so he started inflating the value of our trade-in. It was worth about $500, but we ended up getting $3,500 in credit for it. The dealer finally got the whole package deal to within $50 of what we had saved. We stuck to our guns, stayed with the bottom line (total value, not monthly payments), and got what we never dreamed we could own.

Another slow period that can afford savings is in December. Most people are spending their money on other things that month. January is also slow as people reevaluate their budgets. Early April and May are good times for deals, as people are using their money for tax payments, not cars.

If you can't wait that long to buy a car, you can also try shopping at the end of any month. Many dealers have monthly quotas, and if they haven't met them yet, they are more willing to sell at a low profit. Often manufacturers will offer big cash rebates or financing incentives on slow-moving models. Sometimes the entire industry goes through a slump, and you can get the exact car you want at a bargain price.

Another way to get a good deal is to watch the dealer advertisements in the newspaper. To lure customers in, dealers offer one or two basic vehicles at a low price. They hope you will come in and want a fancier model. The law requires them to print the vehicle ID number in the ad so that no bait and switch is taking place. We saw a Toyota pickup truck offered at $1,500 below normal cost. We called the day the ad appeared to verify that the truck was still there. We were there by dinnertime. We had no time to get to our savings account, so we took their financing and paid it off the next month.

Haggle-Free Car Buying

Some new car dealerships have gone to haggle-free selling. Saturn pioneered this approach, but now a similar one-price-sticker approach for other new cars is on the scene. AutoNation USA is a nationwide chain of dealerships, based in Fort Lauderdale, Florida, created in 1995 by Wayne Huizinga, founder of Blockbuster Video stores. Like Saturn, each car has a nonnegotiable price.

There are also companies that will actually buy your car for you. These are called car-buying services. What they do is arrange for you to purchase the car of your choice through them. Usually the price you pay is only a few hundred dollars over dealer's invoice, plus fees to ship the car to a local dealership or directly to your home. Sometimes you can make an arrangement to pick up the car at the headquarters of the buying service. One such service is Nationwide Auto Brokers (*www.nationwide-auto.com*).

*B*UYING A USED CAR

If buying a new car is too much of a hassle, or you don't have the money for a new car, try a used car. After all, even if you can avoid the salesperson's traps, your new car will lose about one-fourth its value the moment you drive it off the lot. But buying a used car can present an entirely different set of hazards. The main difficulty, of course, is that unless you know the complete history of the used car you're interested in buying, you may simply be acquiring a whole set of problems the previous owner dumped the car to be free of. It may have be. n in an accident that is not easily detectable but that negatively affects the car's performance, safety, and durability. It may be a lemon. Its warranty may be nearly expired or expired.

Research the make and the model's history. Some years were filled with safety and mechanical problems for certain models and should be avoided. For example, when we wanted to buy a used Plymouth Voyager (or Dodge Caravan) we found that there were a few years that this model didn't have a good reputation. After that the problems were fixed. Read up on that model you like at the library. Ask the reference librarian for the *Consumer Digest Car Buying Guide* and the *Consumer Reports* annual car buying issue. These will also list the annual maintenance cost for each type of car. Call the National Highway Traffic Safety Administration (NHTSA) to see if that model has ever had any recalls for safety defects (800-424-9393 or *www.nhtsa.dot.gov*).

One way around these potential problems is to ask if you can have the car for long enough to have it thoroughly inspected by a mechanic. You may have to spend a few dollars to have this done, but you could end up saving yourself a big headache later on. My mechanic charges $100 for this service.

To investigate the history of a used car, all you need is the VIN (vehicle identification number) of the car. This is found on the dashboard. With this you can find out if the car has been in a bad accident or if the title to the car is actually owned by the person selling it to you. You can get a VIN report online through *www.edmunds.com, www.carprices.com, http://carfax.com,* or *www.autoweb.com.* There is usually a $15 fee for the service.

Another thing to think about when buying a used car is that finance rates are often higher than for new cars—sometimes as much as two or three percentage points. Also, you may not be able to get financing for as many months as on a new car. Of course, if you buy a used car from a private party, you will either need to pay cash for it or have financing set up in advance.

If you are buying your used car from a dealer, remember that their main emphasis is going to be on getting that car looking as good as possible. Most car dealerships have detailing departments that specialize in making cars look like new. Although this can result in a dazzling appearance, most of it is cosmetic and has little or nothing to do with making the car run better. And always make sure the purchase price checks out with values of comparable vehicles in the *Kelley Blue Book* (*www.kbb.com*).

Inspect the tires for uneven wear that could indicate alignment problems. If the car has power steering, turn the steering wheel all the way to the left and the right and listen for screeches that indicate a worn belt or power steering pump. Check under the car for leaks. Test-drive it on a bumpy road and listen for rattles or vibrations and other noises. Test the brakes, making sure they don't screech or pull the car to one side.

Other things to check for:

- Badly worn pedals or newly replaced pedals are a sign of heavily used brakes and clutch. It shows that other parts of the car have been heavily used as well.
- Windshield wiper scratches, tears in upholstery or carpet, and badly worn tires show a general neglect by the owner. If she neglected those areas, the rest of the car was probably neglected as well.
- Look for oil change stickers on the doorjamb or windshield. If they are missing, proper maintenance may have been neglected.
- Check for repair work done. Ripples, bumps, or waves in the body and slight discoloration in the paint can indicate extensive bodywork. (This may not rule out a car, but you need to know how sound the frame and structure are. We had a Honda that was demolished both from the rear and the front, bending the frame. It was unrepairable, according to our insurance company. Several months later, we found out that the car had been sold to a woman who never knew its accident history. She had an unsafe car.)
- Mold or discoloration around windows and on the carpeting. The window seals may leak.

- Check the oil dipstick. White oil or bubbles indicates expensive repairs.
- Turn the steering wheel while it is parked. Too much play (more than two inches) indicates repairs are needed.

One way to reduce the hassle of buying a used car is to go through one of the used-car superstore chains, such as Auto-Nation USA or CarMax. These companies feature noncommissioned sales teams and haggle-free pricing, much like Saturn does. The cars have been thoroughly inspected, with fluids and filters changed, worn parts replaced, and minor damages repaired. They have one- to three-month warranties, and they can be returned for a full refund within five to seven days. There are hundreds of these dealerships within the AutoNation USA chain all across the nation.

Something else to consider is buying a used car from a rental car agency. As usual, there is an upside and a downside to this approach. The upside is that you will get a car that has been adequately maintained; it likely will have no major mechanical problems. The downside is that many people who rent cars are rather rough on them. Also, these cars tend to have higher mileage than other used cars, and it is not as easy to get a good deal on one of them.

$\mathcal{U}$SING THE INTERNET

If you are online, the Internet can be a useful tool in helping you make a car-buying decision either for a new or used car. There are a number of sites that will give you helpful information. You can find out such things as dealer invoices, what the actual cost of accessory packages is to dealers, reviews of cars, rankings of cars in various categories according to size and class, handling characteristics, resale values, price ranges for used cars according to mileage and condition, and more. Below is a list of a few of these sites.

Internet Car Buying

Company	Web Address	Features
Auto-by-Tel	*www.autobytel.com*	Comparison shop, get offers from local dealers
AutoPricing	*www.autopricing.com*	Dealer invoice on most models
Auto Web	*www.autoweb.com*	New and used cars, lists for sale by make and model
CarPoint	*www.carpoint.com*	Displays all options for a car and adds up the MSRP (manufacturer's suggested retail price) for you.
Dealer Net	*www.dealernet.com*	New and used cars, search by model, photos, and specs
Trader	*www.traderonline.com*	Listing of used cars
Kelley Blue Book	*www.kbb.com*	Lists all current values on new and used cars
Edmunds New Car Prices	*www.edmunds.com*	Total car shopping advice: reviews new cars for safety, road test information, dealer information invoices, advice for negotiating (also available in book form at libraries and stores)
Black Book Official New-Car Invoice Guide		Book available in libraries and stores, complete auto invoices on new cars

COST OF REPAIRS VS. FREQUENCY OF REPAIRS

Before you make a final decision about buying a car, you may want to look into the issue of cost of repairs versus frequency of repairs. These may sound like the same thing, but they're actually different. Cost of repairs means how much you will have to pay to have your car repaired. Generally speaking, the more expensive the car, the more it costs for any particular repair. This is because higher priced cars often have more sophisticated parts and engineering.

Frequency of repairs means how often your car will have to be in the shop to be fixed. Generally speaking, less expensive cars will have more frequent repairs, although the cost of any single repair might be less. Thus, cost of repairs versus frequency of repairs is often a trade-off. And in many cases you may actually end up spending less money on repairs for a more expensive car. In any case, it is wise to consult one of the consumer magazine guides, such as *Consumer Reports,* for repair and maintenance figures to see which cars have the best track records.

SAFETY

Tremendous advances in safety have been made in the automobile industry in the past few decades. Such things as side-impact panels, airbags, seat belts and shoulder harnesses, antilock braking systems, and radial tires were unheard of fifty years ago. Nevertheless, no car traveling at a high speed on the highway—no matter how many safety features it has and how well it is built—is a completely safe environment. If you have a head-on collision with another car, and both cars are going fifty-five miles per hour, it is like hitting a brick wall at 110 miles per hour.

Once again, in the area of safety, there are trade-offs. For example, the better a car handles, the greater chance you might have of avoiding a collision. Yet often the cars that handle best—sports cars—are the least safe if an accident occurs. Sport utility vehicles are some of the most ruggedly built cars, often on truck platforms, but they typically do not handle very well.

RESOURCES

Annechino, Daniel M. *How to Buy the Most Car for the Least Money: Negotiate the Lowest Possible Price for a New Car Every Time.* Nal/ Dutton, 1993.

Blazak, Robert M. *Carbuying 101: How to Buy a Car With the Change in Your Ashtray.* Rainbow Books, 1997.

Edgerton, Jerry. *Car Shopping Made Easy: Buying or Leasing New or Used.* Warner Books, 1997.

Elliston, Bob. *What Car Dealers Won't Tell You: The Insider's Guide to Buying or Leasing a New or Used Car.* Nal/Dutton, 1996.

Eskeldson, Mark. *What Car Dealers Don't Want You to Know.* Plume, 1996.

Haynes, John. *The Haynes Used Car Buyer's Guide.* Haynes Publications, 1996.

Hazleton, Lesley. *Everything Women Always Wanted to Know About Cars But Didn't Know Who to Ask.* Main Street Books, 1995.

Intellichoice Staff. *Complete Car Cost Guide—2002.* Intellichoice, Inc., 2002.

Leon, Burke, and Stephanie Leon. *The Insider's Guide to Buying a New or Used Car.* Betterway Books, 2000.

Levy, Daniel. *Automobile Aerobics: Exercise Your Right to Trim Thousands off the Price of Your Next Automobile and Make the Dealership Sweat!* Tennyson Publishing, 1996.

Parrish, Darrell B. *The Car Buyer's Art: How to Beat the Salesman at His Own Game.* Book Express, 1997.

———. *Used Cars: How to Buy One.* Artesia, 1995.

Sennert, Ronald, and Barbara Sennert. *How to Save $9,000 on Your Next Car or Van.* Proud American Publishing, 1991.

Stargel, Sky. *The Blue Book of Car-Buying Secrets.* Best Cellar Books, 1993.

CHAPTER FOURTEEN

Car Maintenance: Making Your Car Last

The part of the car that causes the most accidents is the nut that holds the steering wheel.

—Anonymous

$ $ $

One of the biggest budget busters is a car repair. And yet in order to get full value from your car, it is essential that you maintain it properly. Car owners spend $70 million each year on auto maintenance. That means that the average American is spending $500 per year on car repairs. This is easy to imagine since the average repair runs $75 per hour. Because every car is bound to need repairs, all you can do is be prepared. One way to prepare is to create a savings account to which you contribute monthly for this impending expense. Another way to prepare is to become knowledgeable about cars and how they work.

The leading causes of breakdowns are running out of gas, cooling system problems, and tire problems. Most of these can be avoided by preventive maintenance. By periodically checking for proper coolant levels, inspecting tires for uneven wear or cracking, and keeping gas tanks filled, we would have fewer car problems.

To check your coolant levels, look under the hood for the water reservoir. Make sure it is full. If not, add coolant. Coolant can be purchased at most quick-stop stores located at gas stations, discount stores, and auto parts stores.

Changing your car's oil and oil filter are fairly simple as well. For an excellent explanation of how to change the oil yourself, read the detailed description in *Women Home Alone* by Patricia Sprinkle (Zondervan, 1996). Here is a brief checklist of safety tips to keep in mind:

- Know the proper disposal of waste oil in your area (call the city or county for details).
- Avoid prolonged contact of the oil with the skin.
- Don't use thinners or gasoline to clean the oil off surfaces.
- Use waterless hand cleaners for washing hands.

REGULAR MAINTENANCE

Regular car maintenance checks are like brushing and flossing your teeth. Those extra steps prevent wear that causes breakdowns. Don't rely on the indicator light on the dashboard to tell you when something is wrong and needs repair. If that light goes on, damage has already started. Here is a basic list of items to check on your car and how often to check them. Some of these recommendations may differ from what you have heard in the past. These are based on recommendations of several mechanics who feel the "typical" suggestions are not needed.

Car Maintenance Checklist

Item	*Frequency*
Check engine oil levels	once per month
Change oil	5,000 miles*
Replace oil filter	each oil change
Check power steering fluid	once per month
Check brake fluid levels	once per month
Replace spark plugs	30,000 miles
Replace timing belt	60,000–90,000 miles
Air filter replacement	15,000 miles
Check tire pressure	once per month

*The standard recommendation of every 3,000 miles is for heavily used vehicles such as taxis, trucks, etc.

Check tire wear	once per month
Check battery contacts	once per month
Check coolant levels	once per month
Replace brake pads	if pads are $\frac{1}{16}$" or less thick
Replace brake fluid	when you replace brake pads
Replace hoses	50,000–100,000 miles
Replace shocks and struts	100,000 miles or more*
Coolant flush	every other year
Maintain air-conditioner	only if there is a problem

Another thing to remember, especially if you plan on keeping your car for a long time, is to have it washed regularly. This is especially important in areas that have harsh winters where salt is put on road surfaces. Since salt has a corrosive effect on metal, you should wash your car often in the winter, even if it is only going to get dirty again right away. Remember, it is much easier to fix an engine than to repair a car that has rust all over it.

$\mathcal{B}$UYING NEW TIRES

I hate it when it's time for new tires. It's an expense that drains most of my car maintenance fund, and it's a pain to do. There are some better ways to buy tires other

Tire Safety Kit

Since tires are one of the main causes of roadside emergencies, having some handy tools to prevent mishaps is a good idea. The tire industry has put a kit together that may help you. For $4, you can get a kit containing:

- a pressure gauge
- a tread depth gauge
- four tire valve caps
- a consumer tire guide

To get this kit, send a check to:
Tire Industry Safety Council
P.O. Box 3147
Medina, OH 44258

The organization also offers free reading material on tire safety if you send them a self-addressed, stamped envelope with your request. To see what else is offered, visit their Web site: *http://autopedia.com/TireSchool/order.html.*

---

*If someone says your car needs new struts, do the bounce test. Push down on the corner of the car and release. If the car bounces two to three times, that's okay. If it bounces longer, it needs new struts.

than going to the local tire dealer or car repair center. Before you buy, check out tires by mail order. Mail-order prices are usually 35 percent less than retail. Even with the added expenses of shipping costs, mounting and balancing fees, and the disposal of the old tires, the cost still often comes out ahead.

Here are some tire mail-order retailers:

Teletire	(800) 835-8473	
	(714) 250-8355	(in California)
Tire Rack	(800) 428-8355	*www.tirerack.com*
Discount Tire Direct	(800) 589-6789	*www.discounttiredirect.com*

ASOLINE

I have had more conversations over what type of gas is best, what is needed, and what should be avoided. And each discussion ends with a different conclusion. So after doing some additional research, I have concluded the following about gasoline:

- Hi-octane gas is a waste of money. You only need it if your car knocks or pings. Most cars are designed to work on low-octane gas.
- The average car uses 17 percent less gas at 55 MPH than at 65 MPH.
- Fuel additives are not necessary. They don't improve the performance of your car, and they can cause problems for some cars.
- Don't overfill the gas tank. The gas needs some space for the vapor. If you top off the tank, you can cause damage by not leaving that space.
- Driving in low gear when a higher gear is available will use up to twice as much gas.
- Under-inflated tires can use up to 15 percent more gasoline.
- Fast acceleration will use excess gas.
- Revving the engine uses excess gas.
- Idling for longer than one minute wastes fuel. Turning off the car and restarting is less damaging than continuing to idle. Idling alone can run up a $90 gas bill per year for some cars.
- The type of road you drive on affects gas mileage: pothole-

filled roads use up 15 percent more gas than smooth-paved roads, and loose-gravel roads use up 35 percent more gas than paved roads.

- Don't downshift instead of braking. It is cheaper to replace brakes than a transmission.

WHEN YOU NEED HELP

Chances are that you will need someone to repair your car at some time or another. Even those who tinker with their cars will need another mechanic under the hood occasionally. Knowing how to spot a good mechanic is key to avoiding being ripped off. (The next section will help with that area.) Even when a good mechanic is in your employ, here are some things that can help make the whole transaction smoother.

- Ask for recommendations from friends. Why do they use that person?
- Be specific with your needs. Tell the mechanic in detail what the problem is and what you want repaired.
- When you get an estimate, don't feel pressured into agreeing to the work right away. Say that you need to talk it over with your spouse or check your bank account first. Whatever reason you give, use that time to research what others would charge for the same work. You'll be amazed at the variety of fees.
- Read up on that specific area of service. See if you think the mechanic's proposed repair sounds reasonable. You'll find books at the library that discuss each area of the car and what is reasonable. See the resource section at the end of this chapter for a starter list.
- If you have trouble with the service received on your car, stand up for yourself. Go back and explain what you wanted and what actually happened. If you cannot resolve it directly, contact the Consumer Protection division of the office of the Attorney General in your state's capitol.

How to Spot a Good Mechanic

A government study claims that about one-third of every dollar spent on car repairs was for unnecessary work. You don't need to know how to fix a car to know when a repair is needed. But there are some ways to avoid the traps and pitfalls of bad mechanics.

First, arm yourself with knowledge. Know some of the basics of how cars work. For example, a common scam is being told that your brakes need replacing. Knowledge about brakes can help you avoid it: Find out what percentage of wear is left on the brakes and read in your owner's manual what the recommended level is for replacement. Or call a dealer that sells your make of car and ask what

Car Repair Show

Do you wish you knew more about how your car runs or what the news is on the latest car models? For these and other useful tips for the car owner, tune in to a national radio talk show every Saturday. *The C.A.R. Show* is live and takes callers (888–8CARSHOW) for two hours from 9–11 A.M. (EST). For more information, or to e-mail your question, check out its Web site: *www.thecarshow.com.*

is recommended.

Other ways to become knowledgeable about cars are to take a community college or community adult education course on basic auto repair, read your owner's manual, read introductory books on car repair written for the novice (there are a few recommended in the back of this chapter), or have a mechanic friend explain a few things to you.

Chances are good that you will find good mechanics at most car repair facilities. To make sure, check for a rating of some type, such as a AAA endorsement or affiliation. Call the Better Business Bureau to check up on the garage. Finally, to help you identify those that are good, here are some additional tips.

A Bad Mechanic Might:	*A Good Mechanic Will:*
object to your questions	give you a written estimate
charge you to examine the car	guarantee his work
be rude if you suggest a solution	give you a copy of the detailed
most likely be found on inter-	estimate
state highway exits (few peo-	
ple come back to complain)	

*F*INAL TIPS

Keep a logbook in the glove compartment of your car. Write down all types of services that you have done on the car. You won't be able to remember everything that you do. A log is helpful when selling the car because you can prove the care that you took. Keeping track of gas mileage in the log is also helpful. When you see the mileage dropping, have the car inspected for why that is happening. It may indicate a problem.

When owners of cars that had at least 150,000 miles on them were asked what they did to preserve the life of the car, they all had the following habits in common:

- Changed oil and oil filters regularly.
- Took care of minor repairs when they arose.
- Followed the manufacturer's recommended service schedule.

Happy motoring!

RESOURCES

Burgoyne, J. Robert. *You Can Cut Car Costs.* Maryland FYI, 1993.

Cerullo, Bob. *What's Wrong With My Car?* Dutton/Plume, 1993.

Consumer Reports Staff. *Consumer Report's Used Car Buying Guide, 2001.* Consumer Reports, 2001.

Fariello, Sal. *The People's Car Book.* St. Martin, 1992.

Fendell, Bob. *How to Make Your Car Last a Lifetime.* Holt, Rinehart, and Winston, 1981.

Fremon, George, and Suzanne Fremon. *Why Trade It In? Keep Your Car Trouble-Free.* Liberty Publishing, 1991.

Glickman, Arthur P. *Avoiding Auto Repair Rip-Offs.* Consumer Reports Books, 1995.

Goulter, Vic, and Barbara Goulter. *How to Keep Your Car Mechanic Honest.* Scarborough House, 1990.

Schultz, Mort. *Keep Your Car Running Practically Forever: An Easy Guide to Routine Care and Maintenance.* Consumer Reports Books, 1991.

Sikorsky, Robert. *Drive It Forever: Secrets to Long Automobile Life.* ATG Media, 1998.

———. *Rip-Off Tip-Offs: Winning the Auto Repair Game.* Tab Books, 1990.

Stevenson, Chris. *Auto Repair Shams and Scams: How to Avoid Getting Ripped Off.* Putnam, 1990.

Magliozzi, Tom, and Ray Magliozzi. *Car Talk.* Soundelux Publishing, 2001.

Morton, B. A. *How Women Win the Auto Repair Game: A Consumer Survival Guide.* Carsmart Publications, 1996.

Sclar, Deanna. *Auto Repair for Dummies.* IDG Books, 1999.

Sprinkle, Patricia. *Women Home Alone.* Zondervan, 1996.

CHAPTER FIFTEEN

I Can't Take It Anymore! — Consumer Rights

Take time to deliberate; but when the time for action arrives, stop thinking and go in.

—Andrew Jackson

$ $ $

*N*othing is more annoying than paying for something and not having it work properly. Have you ever bought an item that broke within a short period of time? Or perhaps it never worked properly from the beginning, but the manufacturer claims it is working fine. Then this chapter is for you.

The first thing consumers need to understand before trying to resolve a problem is what their rights are. This is what you will lean on when the other side starts to push back or resists your attempts at correcting the situation. It is also necessary to know if you are barking up the wrong tree. There is nothing more embarrassing than complaining, only to have it pointed out that you were in the wrong all along. This scene reminds me of the old *Saturday Night Live* television program skit with Gilda Radner portraying Roseanne Roseannadanna who complains and makes a public fool of herself, later having to say, "Never mind."

THE CONSUMER'S RESPONSIBILITY

Every consumer is responsible for reading the instructions, reading labels, asking around for advice, and getting the right price. No one else can be blamed for problems in any of these areas. When I worked at a small computer start-up company, the customer service department consisted of one person. She said that 80 percent of her calls came from people who didn't bother to read the directions and wanted her to tell them what to do. All of the other legitimate calls could not get through to her because those who wouldn't take responsibility for reading the directions jammed the lines.

Pricing is another area in which the consumer must accept responsibility. No one else can be blamed for your not getting the best price. I'm not talking about the times when an expensive item goes on sale at the same store within a few weeks of your purchase. In this case, sometimes you can get the difference refunded since it was from the same store. I'm referring to the consumer who wants to return something because she found she could get it through mail order much cheaper. That is the consumer's fault, not the retailer's.

COMPLAINTS

Complaints should be based on good information. That information is a right of yours as the consumer. You have the right to be informed of safety features, your choices, and you have the right to be heard and have your complaints addressed.

In order to complain effectively, there are a few things you need to do. If you complain in person, by telephone, or by mail, your approach will be a little different in each case. But before I go into the details of an effective complaint, I want to editorialize a little bit.

The Art of Complaining

Complaining does not have to be a battle. Sometimes it may turn into one, but I always try to make that the last resort. I have friends who believe that you have to get ugly to get anywhere. They have these victorious war stories to demonstrate their point. I have a different philosophy.

Whenever I run into problems, I look at it as an opportunity for something good to happen to us. We may have to work at getting the solution we want, but we usually benefit from the mishap in some way. I call this the Silver Lining Approach. One of my favorite examples was a sleeper sofa that we bought from a sofa manufacturing company. We had it manufactured for us from showroom models, fabric samples they provided, and other details from their warehouse. The couch was supposed to take six to eight weeks to make. After nine weeks, we complained that it still wasn't ready (they ran out of fabric at the warehouse and were waiting on a shipment). For this complaint, we got free fabric protection added to the couch. After two or three more weeks of waiting, we called again. This time we were appeased with a superior quality mattress and springs in the foldout sleeper. After a few more weeks, we were pacified with free delivery. Finally, when the couch arrived, we had a superior product for the price of an inconvenience.

Everyone feels the price of inconvenience differently. Some cannot tolerate the inconvenience and get very upset by it. Others, like myself, look at it as an opportunity for a blessing. If you expect otherwise, frustration will be with you often. If you look at it as a way to get something else, you can have some fun with it.

How to Complain

How you complain can affect the outcome. Complaining in person and politely will usually produce the best results. When it doesn't, seeing a supervisor, writing a letter, or getting a consumer advocate involved may be required. Try these ideas in the order they are written the next time you need to tackle a consumer problem.

Complaining in Person

Most success stories in consumer rights come from those who complained in person. People like the personal touch, and a body in front of them sometimes intimidates clerks. Store personnel have their own tricks to try to combat the complaining consumer. Some may try *intimidation*. They will try to make you feel incompetent or diminished. Others may give you the *brush-off* or *turn the tables* on you and say that it's your fault. Don't react to these ploys and fall into their trap. Restate your problem and desired solution. If they persist in their attitude, go find their supervisor.

If you plan on complaining in person, do the following:

- Bring the item in the original packaging, if possible.
- Bring the sales receipt, invoice, or proof of purchase (see note below).
- Be polite.
- Try to start with the original salesperson.
- If the salesperson cannot resolve the problem, go up the chain of command.
- Clearly state the essential information such as date of purchase, what was purchased, the problem you encountered, and how you want it resolved (see note on resolution below).
- Do not be demanding.
- Document whom you spoke to, the date and time, and the resolution (you may need it for a future resolution).
- Write a thank-you letter to the salesperson about his/her help in how the matter was resolved.

Note on receipts: If you no longer have the receipt or cannot find it, do not despair. Be honest with the salesperson, but be persistent in the need for a solution to your problem. Remember that couch I told you about? Nine months later the frame snapped inside one of the arms. When we bought it, we were told we had a lifetime warranty on the couch's construction, so we tried to take advantage of this. The company originally would not help us because we could not locate the receipt or a sales number. Our name and address was no longer in their system, so we had no proof that it was their couch. I continued to politely call the sales agent that currently worked there, insisting that we needed this fixed. After four months of calling, she relented and wrote up a repair order. In this case, polite persistence paid off.

Note on resolution: Many consumers don't determine what they want as a resolution to the problem. Make sure you think in advance about what you want and clearly state it at the end of your presentation of the facts. If you don't, the merchant gets to decide what to do for you.

Complaining by Telephone

Sometimes complaining in person is not practical or possible, such as when you have moved away from the area or have difficulty getting around town. Telephoning can be very effective, however, if done properly. Here are some tips:

- Be polite.
- Try to talk with the original salesperson.
- If you don't know the salesperson's name, or the salesperson cannot resolve the problem, go up the chain of command.
- Clearly state the essential information, such as date of purchase, what was purchased, the problem you encountered, and how you want it resolved (see note on previous page).
- Do not be demanding.
- Document whom you spoke to, the date and time, and the resolution (you may need it for a future resolution).
- Write a thank-you letter to the salesperson about his/her help in how the matter was resolved.

Complaining by Mail

There are times when you cannot reach the company in person or by phone and have to write. And sometimes you have tried these other tactics only to get no satisfaction, leaving you with writing to the company headquarters as a last resort. If you have to take this route, keep these things in mind:

- Be patient. Your issue may take a few months to get to the right person.
- Write a business format letter, including your complete address, phone number, and date.
- Avoid handwritten notes if possible.
- Include information on the item purchased, full description with model number, if possible, and copies of the sales receipt or proof-of-purchase.
- Clearly ask for what you want to resolve the issue.
- Be polite.
- Keep copies of your letter.
- Send by certified mail, if possible. This gives you proof it was received and requires the company to respond to it.

- If your first letter is not answered, send a second letter, stating what you will do if this one is not addressed. (See "What Do You Do Next?")

Sometimes it pays to let a company know of your dissatisfaction with something that happened, even if you don't have an item to exchange or return. I have written explaining how something was unsatisfactory and received free stuff. I wrote to United Airlines about a series of mishaps that happened on my last trip with them. None of the mishaps were enormous, just annoying. They responded with a $75 gift certificate. When I purchased a bag of prewashed lettuce, it smelled musty but looked fine. I wrote the company and told them about it. I received five coupons for free lettuce.

What Do You Do Next?

If the matter is not being resolved to your satisfaction after taking the above steps, then try these tips:

- Contact your state consumer protection agency. The number is located in your phone book under government agencies. They can help by writing to the company on your behalf, providing information on consumer law, and may help in court proceedings, if necessary.
- Contact the Better Business Bureau.
- Contact the Federal Trade Commission.
- Contact a consumer advocate—often found at radio stations, television stations, and newspapers. This can be very effective, as the companies do not want public bad press.
- Contact a consumer action panel. Two industries that I know of have set these up for consumers; one is for major appliances and the other is for cars. If you have a problem with your item and cannot get it resolved with the retailer, try going to one of these panels:

Major Appliances Consumer Action Program
    20 N. Wacker Circle, Suite 1550
    Chicago, IL 60606
    (800) 621-0477

AUTOCAP: National Automobile Dealer's Association (NADA)
    8400 Westpark Dr.

McLean, VA 22102
(800) 252-6232
www.nada.org

- Give your credit card company a call. Some companies will help you resolve your problem with the manufacturer or retailer if you used their card to purchase the item.
- As a last resort, you can sue in small claims court or regular court, depending on the dollar value of the claim. Make sure you have followed all of the recommended steps before taking this route and that you have all documentation proving that all steps were taken to prevent a court claim.

WHAT ARE YOUR RIGHTS?

The Federal Trade Commission (FTC) was established to regulate consumer transactions. It focuses on deceptive practices, false advertising, phony investment schemes, and bogus health claims. It has established some rules, such as the Funeral Rule (requires funeral homes to disclose all prices and information about their goods and services and that coffins do not have to be purchased from the home to have a service or burial there), the Cooling Off Rule (gives a buyer three days to cancel a sale of $25 or more if the sale is made other than at the seller's place of business), and the Used Car Rule (requires the dealer to post warranty and other information). Some of the rules that they have established are more encompassing, as described below.

Advertising Rules

We are all familiar with ads: they get our attention and draw us into the store. Let's look at what ads can and cannot do.

- Advertising is not the same as an offer.
- An offer is legally binding and must have four points: who is making the offer, the subject matter of the offer, quantity of items in the offer, and price.
- Bait and switch is illegal. (This is where an advertised item is not available and never was.) Make sure you can see the advertised model and compare it to others being offered.

Mail Order and Telephone Sales Rules

These rules cover anything advertised or ordered by mail, phone, fax, or computer.

- Goods must be shipped within the specified time period. If no time period was specified, then it must be mailed within thirty days of the order.
- If the time frame cannot be met, the merchant must notify you of the delay and offer a refund if desired.
- No substitute items have to be accepted by you.
- Unordered merchandise is to be considered a gift, and there is no obligation to pay. If a bill arrives for unordered merchandise, this is fraud.
- Paying with a credit card helps resolve disputes more easily. The credit card company sometimes helps you resolve the issue.
- To remove your name from national direct mail lists, write to DMA Mail Preference Service, P.O. Box 9008, Farmingdale, NY 11735-9008. You can register online for a $5 fee (*www.thedma.org/cgi/offmailinglistdave*).
- To remove yourself from telephone marketing lists, write to DMA Telephone Preference Service, P.O. Box 9014, Farming-

Credit Card Advantages

There are some advantages to using a credit card for some purchases. Check to see if your credit card company has any of these features.

- Travel insurance: if you die or are disabled by an accident that involves a public carrier (planes, buses, trains, ships).
- Warranty extension: Some card companies will extend the original warranty of some items, usually those that have long original warranties.
- Purchase protection: Accidental damage or theft of a recently purchased item is sometimes covered by the card if the purchase was made with the card and the damage takes place within a certain amount of time from the date of purchase.

Note: Don't buy credit card insurance. These policies protect you from excessive charges in case you lose the card. They are not necessary, since federal law limits your liability to $50 if you notify the card company immediately.

dale, NY 11735-9014. You can register online for a $5 fee (*www.thedma.org/cgi/offtelephonedave#howto*).

• If you have a mail-order matter that cannot be resolved with the recommended suggestions, try contacting these people for help: Direct Marketing Association (DMA), Suite 1100, 1111 19th Street, NW, Washington, DC 20036.

Warranties

A warranty is a statement about the manufacturer's confidence in his product. The better quality products usually have a superior warranty. There are two types: expressed warranties and implied warranties. Here's the difference:

Note on Warranties

You do not have to return the warranty cards that are included with the products you purchase. These are not intended to validate your warranty but rather to notify you of future product upgrades or recalls. Retaining your receipt is just as effective.

• Expressed warranties: This is a promise to back up any warranty that is written or given orally by the seller.
• Implied warranties: These are automatic warranties, supported by law. These warranties imply that an item is fit for what it was sold for. For example, the shirt must be able to withstand washing, and the milk carton must have milk in it that is drinkable. This warranty also assumes that an item will last for a reasonable amount of time. The store manager or manufacturer will determine that time.

Whatever the warranty is, you must be able to read it, the language must be plain and clear, the address of the company must be printed on it, and the length of the warranty and parts covered must be declared.

Exceptions: In some places you will find the implied warranty to be extremely hampered. Thrift stores, boutiques, and consignment shops either have very limited time periods for returning items or they expect you to check the item out first and take some responsibility for your choice.

If you have trouble with an item on warranty, try to do the following:

- Return the item in its original shipping container (keep those boxes!).
- Don't try to fix it yourself or open the device. This voids most warranties.
- Keep good records and receipts.

RESOURCES

Kiplinger. *Know Your Legal Rights.* Kiplinger, 2001.

Lieberman, Marc R. *Your Rights As a Consumer: Legal Tips for Savvy Purchases of Goods, Services, and Credit.* Career Press, 1994.

Marsh, Gene. *Consumer Law in a Nutshell.* West Publishing, 1999.

McCohan, Donna. *Get What You Pay for or Don't Pay at All: Consumer Resource Manual.* Crown Trade Paperbacks, 1994.

Portnoy, J. Elias. *Let the Seller Beware!—The Complete Consumer Guide to Getting Your Money's Worth.* Macmillan, 1990.

Ross, Linda. *The Smart Consumer's Book of Questions.* Chicago Review Press, 1996.

Sack, Steven Mitchell. *Don't Get Taken.* Alliance House, 2001.

Singer, Arlene, and Karen Parment. *Take It Back!—The Art of Returning Almost Anything.* National Press Books, 1992.

Here is a list of resources that I used in research for this book or recommend that you research for further information on a particular subject. I hope it helps you on your journey to frugality!

FRUGAL LIVING

Bredenberg, Jeff. *Beat the System: 1,200 Tips for Coming Out on Top in Every Deal and Transaction.* Berkley Publishing Group, 1999.

Dacyczyn, Amy. *The Complete Tightwad Gazette.* Random House, 1999.

Horowitz, Shel. *The Penny-Pinching Hedonist: How to Live Like Royalty With a Peasant's Pocketbook.* AWM Book, 1995.

Hunt, Mary. *The Complete Cheapskate: How to Break Free From Money Worries Forever Without Sacrificing Your Quality of Life.* Broadman & Holman, 1998.

———. *Tiptionary.* Broadman & Holman, 1997.

Kay, Ellie. *How to Save Money Every Day.* Bethany House, 2001.

Levine, Karen. *Keeping Life Simple: 7 Guiding Principles, 500 Tips & Ideas.* Storey Publishing, 1996.

McBride, Tracey. *Frugal Luxuries by the Seasons: Celebrate the Holidays With Elegance and Simplicity on Any Income.* Bantam Doubleday Dell, 2000.

McCoy, Jonni. *Miserly Moms: Living on One Income in a Two-Income Economy.* Bethany House, 2001.

Miller, Mark W. *The Complete Idiot's Guide to Being a Cheapskate.* Alpha Books, 1999.

Moore, Melodie. *The Frugal Almanac.* Signet Books, 1997.

Paris, James L. *Absolutely Amazing Ways to Save Money on Everything.* Harvest House, 1999.

Potter, Michelle A. *The Complete Saving Source Catalog: A Guide to Saving the Earth and Money.* RIMA World Press, 1997.

Quinn, Hope Stanley, and Lyn Miller-Lachmann. *Downsized but Not Defeated: The Family Guide to Living on Less.* Andrews McMeel, 1997.

Reid, Lisa. *Raising Kids With Just a Little Cash.* Ferguson-Carol Publishers, 1996.

Roberts, William. *How to Save Money on Just About Everything.* Paladin Press, 2002.

Roth, Larry. *The Best of Living Cheap News: Practical Advice on Saving Money and Living Well.* McGraw Hill, 1996.

Roth, Larry, ed. *The Simple Life: Thoughts on Simplicity, Frugality, and Living Well.* Berkley Press, 1998.

Simmons, Lee, and Barbara Simmons. *Penny Pinching: How to Lower Your Everyday Expenses Without Lowering Your Standard of Living.* Bantam Books, 1999.

Taylor-Hough, Deborah. *A Simple Choice: A Practical Guide to Saving Your Time, Money, and Sanity.* Champion Press, 2000.

Zalewski, Angie, and Deana Ricks. *Cheap Talk With the Frugal Friends: Over 600 Tips, Tricks, and Creative Ideas for Saving Money.* Starburst Publishing, 2001.

GROCERY SAVINGS AND COOKING INEXPENSIVE MEALS

Barfield, Rhonda. *Eat Healthy for $50 a Week: Feed Your Family Nutritious, Delicious Meals for Less.* Kensington Publishing, 1996.

Barfield, Rhonda. *Feed Your Family for $12 a Day.* Citadel Press, 2002.

Bond, Jill. *Mega Cooking: A Revolutionary New Plan for Quantity Cooking.* Cumberland House, 2000.

Hunt, Mary. *Cheapskate in the Kitchen: Everything You Need to Know About Creating Fabulous Meals at a Fraction of the Cost!* St. Martin Press, 1997.

Kaysing, Bill. *Eat Well for 99¢ a Meal.* Breakout Productions, 1996.

Kaysing, Bill, and Ruth Kaysing. *The 99¢ a Meal Cookbook.* Breakout Productions, 1996.

Lavigne, R. J. *Cookmiser.* Scrypt Publishing, 2000.

McCoy, Jonni. *Miserly Meals.* Bethany House, 2001.

Tawra, Jean Killam. *Not Just Beans: 50 Years of Frugal Family Favorites.* Not Just Beans, 1999.

Taylor-Hough, Deborah. *Frozen Assets: How to Cook for a Day and Eat for a Month.* Champion Press, 1998.

———. *Frozen Assets Lite and Easy: How to Cook for a Day and Eat for a Month.* Champion Press, 2001.

BARGAIN HUNTING AND YARD SALES

Causey, Kimberly. *The Furniture Factory Outlet Guide.* Home Décor Press, 2002.

Hoff, Al. *Thrift Score: The Stuff, the Method, the Madness.* Harper Perennial, 1997.

King, Trisha, and Deborah Newmark. *Buying Retail Is Stupid! USA: The National Discount Guide to Buying Everything at Up to 80% Off Retail.* McGraw Hill, 2000.

McClurg, R. S. *The Rummager's Handbook: Finding, Buying, Cleaning, Fixing, Using, and Selling Secondhand Treasures.* Storey Books, 1995.

Price, Lisa. *The Best of Online Shopping: The Prices' Guide to Fast and Easy Shopping on the Web.* Ballantine Books, 1999.

Schmeltz, L. R. *The Backyard Money Machine: How to Organize and Operate a Successful Garage Sale.* Silver Streak Publications, 1993.

Schneider, Carolyn. *The Ultimate Consignment and Thrift Store Guide.* Consignment and Thrift Store Publishing, 1998.

Simmons, Sylvia. *The Great Garage Sale Book: How to Run a Garage, Tag, Attic, Barn, or Yard Sale.* Universe.com, 2000.

Weil, Christa. *Secondhand Chic: The Secrets of Finding Fantastic Bargains at Thrift Shops, Consignment Shops, Vintage Shops, and More.* Pocket Books, 1999.

Wells, Dick. *Your Hidden Money!—How to Have Your Own Profitable Yard, Garage, Block, or Estate Sale.* Aztex Corp., 2001.

Chapter 1

1. Darcie Sanders and Martha Bullen, *Staying Home: From Full-Time Professional to Full-Time Parent* (Boston: Little, Brown & Company, 1992), xiv.
2. Andy Dappen, *Shattering the Two-Income Myth* (Brier, Washington: Brier Books, 1997), 40.
3. Sanders and Bullen, 215–16.
4. Donna Otto, *The Stay at Home Mom* (Eugene, Oregon: Harvest House Publishers, 1997), 27–28.
5. Dappen, 8.
6. Sanders and Bullen, 217.
7. Ibid., 222.
8. Ibid., 216.
9. Dappen, 7.

Chapter 2

1. Loriann Hoff Oberlin, *Working at Home While the Kids Are There Too* (Franklin Lakes, New Jersey: Career Press, 1997) 66.

Chapter 4

1. If you would rather buy the eggs readymade, contact FamilyLife Today at (800) 358–6329.

Chapter 9

1. *Federal Reserve Bulletin,* January, 2002, 19–21.
2. *To Owe or Not to Owe,* Special Consumer Survey Report, The Conference Board, Moody's Weekly Financial Report, June 14, 1996.
3. "Consumer Credit: Is a Crunch Coming?" *BusinessWeek,* August 2, 2002.
4. Larry Burkett, *A Guide to Family Budgeting* (1993), 13–25, pamphlet. Used with permission from Crown Financial Ministries, *www.crown.org.*

5. Olivia Millan, *Overcoming Overspending* (New York: Walker & Co., 1995), 18–19.

Chapter 10

1. Jason Schachter, Current Population Reports, U.S. Census Bureau, May 2001.
2. Lynne Schreiber, "Families on the Move in Summer," *The Detroit News,* May 11, 2001.